HHB

TRANSCENDENCE

Seekers and Seers
in the
Age of Thoreau

by

François Specq

A *Directions 21* Book
Series Editor: Randall Conrad

Higganum Hill Books - Higganum, CT

First Edition
First Printing, September 1, 2006

Higganum Hill Books
P.O. Box 666, Higganum, Connecticut 06441-0666
Phone: (860) 345-4103
e-mail: rcdebold@mindspring.com
Web: www.calliope.org/hhb/

The *"Directions 21"* Series is edited by Randall Conrad
Library of Congress Control Number 200622702
ISBN10: 0-9741158-9-4
ISBN13: 978-0-9741158-9-4
Cover: Frederic Edwin Church, *Twilight in the Wilderness* (1860), detail
Frontispiece: William Bradford, *Labrador Coast* (1860).

Library of Congress Cataloging-in-Publication Data

Specq, Francois, 1965-
  Transcendence : seekers and seers in the age of Thoreau / by Francois
Specq. -- 1st ed.
    p. cm. -- (Directions 21)
  Includes bibliographical references.
  ISBN-13: 978-0-9741158-9-4 (alk. paper)
  ISBN-10: 0-9741158-9-4 (alk. paper)
  1. American literature--19th century--History and criticism. 2.
Transcendentalism (New England) 3. Spirituality in literature. 4.
Spirituality in art. 5. Nature in literature. 6. Nature in art. 7. Nature--
Religious aspects. I. Title.
  PS217.T7S74 2006
  810.9'384--dc22

                                        2006022702

Printed in the United States of America
Higganum Hill Books is distributed by Independent Publishers Group
Phone: (800) 888-4741 or Internet: www. ipgbook.com

CONTENTS

Chs. *1, 4, 5, 6, 8, 9 and 10 were translated from the French
By Randall Conrad and James Williston.*

Introduction

The following essays reflect my central interest in the literature and visual arts of Antebellum America. Although they were written as serious academic pieces, their primary claim is not authority and definitiveness: I would prefer to think of them as exercises in thinking. I hope that they have retained part of the excitement of reading and thinking about the works of Thoreau, Emerson, and Melville, as well as those of the artists Frederic Edwin Church and William Bradford. Consequently, they do not attempt to survey or explicitly engage with the voluminous secondary literature on these authors, although they were in no way written in a mood of arrogant ignorance of what past and present colleagues have had to say. Neither are they theoretical in the sense of providing new conceptualizations of literature and literary genres, or of problematising literary history. My primary interest is in how each work of literature changes the way we perceive the world: the literature of Antebellum America was especially concerned with producing renewed and enhanced awareness in its readers.

Although some of the essays deal with famous works by famous writers (Emerson's *Essays*, Thoreau's *Walden*), a fair proportion deals with comparatively neglected works by famous writers: such narratives and short stories as Thoreau's « Chesuncook » or Melville's « The Piazza » and « The Encantadas », as well as these authors' Journals, occupy a minor place in the critical literature. My assumption was that they deserve attention in their own right, and that re-entering the canon through the side doors might provide new insights, and help to expose and clarify some still unarticulated configurations of meaning.

Although we cannot re-create the exact experience of the writers we study, we may try to reconstruct their ways of seeing, not with a view to providing disembodied knowledge, but so as to see through their eyes, so to speak. If postmodernism has made decentering one of its catchwords, my purpose is not to decenter the canon, the authors or their works, but to experience the way they decenter us as readers and human beings, thus helping us expand our consciousness. And what has always fascinated me, what I have found most exhilarating and stimulating, is the attempt to experience decentering in a way that is always singular. In other words, my purpose was not to study this or that theme or topic, but to experience singular works by singular authors and lie open to the way they transform us. This is not to say that these works do shape our perception of reality, but that they provide a powerful counterweight to our easily and rapidly fossilizing worldview. They give momentum to the life of the mind, they keep it going, they preserve mobility and movement.

Acknowledgements

Most of the articles collected here are based on research carried out both in scholarly solitude and in academic circles. They were first presented at various times and places: these primarily included research centers in Lyon (Lieux d'Amérique, University of Lyon 2), and in Paris (Atelier XIXe siècle, and Groupe d'histoire des images, both University of Paris 7), but also the ASLE (Association for the Study of Literature and Environment) biennial conferences, the AFEA (French Association for American Studies) annual conferences, the SANAS (Swiss Association for North American Studies) and SAUTE (Swiss Association of University Teachers of English) biennial conferences. My thinking has benefitted greatly from comments and suggestions by colleagues and friends on such occasions.

Thanks are due to François Brunet, Michel Granger, Philippe Jaworski, and Barton Levi St. Armand, for their constant support, encouragement and stimulation over the years.

I also owe a debt of gratitude to Richard DeBold, who generously offered to publish this book by a French americanist.

I wish to single out Randall Conrad for special thanks. He constantly contributed his patience and his good and good-humored advice to the preparation of the manuscript. Thanks to his expertise in French and the literature of the Antebellum period, his coordination of the translation was constantly thoughtful, and his readings of the articles directly written in English saved me from errors and infelicities of expression.

And finally, thanks and love to Sylvie, and to our children Jean, Marion, Élie and Joachim, for whom researching and writing must have sounded a never-ending task. It is. But they have made it a lot lighter.

Lyon, France.
August 2006.

ix

1

Frederic Church's America

It was Henry David Thoreau's lament in "Chesuncook" (1858) that wild nature was now the haunt of woodcutters more than poets and painters.[1] Thoreau concluded that essay with the idea that a person's life should partake of both civilization *and* wilderness. Around the same time, the painter Frederic Edwin Church, a resident of New York, became seriously interested in the wild nature of Maine. He first visited Mount Katahdin (Thoreau's "Ktaadn") in 1851 and came back on numerous occasions, finally purchasing a parcel of land on the shore of nearby Lake Millinocket where he built a seasonal home he called Rhodora. Church thus spent much of his life in either New York or the wilderness (not only the Maine woods but also the Andes and Labrador). Like Thoreau, he was an avid reader of both Alexander von Humboldt and John Ruskin.

It would be tempting to conclude that Church embodies Thoreau's ideal of the artist in some respects. However, Church's world-view and idea of the artist's role in society were profoundly different from Thoreau's. And Thoreau would probably have felt misgivings in front of the paintings inspired by Church's sojourns in the wild, especially the masterworks of his maturity–*Andes of Ecuador*, *Niagara*, *Heart of the Andes*, *Twilight in the Wilderness*, *The Icebergs*, and *Cotopaxi* (1855-1862). In fact, Thoreau did go to see the first of these, *Andes of Ecuador*, when it was exhibited at the Boston Athenaeum in

---

[1] Thoreau 1972, 120, 155-56. I discuss "Chesuncook" in detail in Chapter 2.

1855.[2] Unfortunately he never recorded his impressions for posterity. My purpose here is not to fill in this blank, but rather to point up some essential aspects of Church's art and thereby shed some light upon Thoreau's as well.

God, Artist and Man

To Church, it should be noted, America meant not just the United States, but the continental whole of North and South America, from the Arctic to the Andes. South America takes on a particular importance with Church, just as it did for both Charles Darwin and Alfred Russel Wallace, as well as for their predecessor Humboldt. The intellectual influence of this great German naturalist-explorer,[3] famous for his South American expeditions at the turn of the nineteenth century, was substantial among Western thinkers prior to the Darwinian revolution, primarily through his *Personal Narrative* and *Cosmos*.[4] Humboldt's chapter on landscape painting in *Cosmos* so struck Church that he followed in the German thinker's footsteps and visited the Andes. From April to October of 1853, Church explored the mountains in Colombia and Ecuador. The excursion resulted in *Andes of Ecuador*, his first mature work, two years later.[5]

Andes of Ecuador typifies Church's art in a number of respects. First, it is a large-scale canvas, 1.22 m by 1.90 m, as are most of Church's subsequent major works. Such great size

---

[2] Church *Andes of Ecuador*, 1855, Reynolds House, Museum of American Art, Winston-Salem, N.C. On Thoreau's visit to the Atheneum, see Richardson 339.

[3] See Laura Dassow Walls, "Humboldt's *Cosmos* and the Birth of the Two Cultures," a paper delivered at the Humboldt 2004 Bicentennial Conference, City University of New York, October 14-16, 2004. (Ed.)

[4] Both these works were in Church's library at Olana and were also read by Thoreau (Sattelmeyer 206-07).

[5] Another visit to the same region in May-August 1857 inspired *Heart of the Andes* (1859).

naturally helps to express and produce an impression of immensity and expansion, and so corresponds to the era's taste for panoramic views. The large-scale canvas becomes an equivalent to the popular panorama, but in the "higher" category of easel-paintings.[6] Second, beyond formal characteristics, what is striking in this painting above all is its religious tenor, its expression of a triumphant faith in a God of light who is revealed in the American wild and spreads his blessing in it just as on the first morning of creation. Thus *Andes of Ecuador* was presented in its time as a "sublime psalm of light"[7] and a manifestation of "God's benediction."[8]

Most of Church's paintings in his mature period thus present us with a transcendent order, symbolized by the radical break between the picture's plane and the viewer. As viewers, we often seem suspended on the edge of an abyss. We are not invited, metaphorically, to step into the field of the painting; instead, we are confronted with a vision, a revelation of divine transcendence. Church's God is not an immanent presence within his Creation, like Ralph Waldo Emerson's "Oversoul," but instead reveals himself through it. Church's world has nothing to do with pantheism, nor with the hint of materialism that attaches to that doctrine. In spite of his Protestantism, Church is closer to Pascal than he is to Spinoza. Church is the painter of transcendence and revelation; orthodox in religion, he

---

[6] On the connection between the panorama as a popular genre and the spectacular form adopted by certain types of American landscape painting in the nineteenth century, see Novak 18-28.

[7] "Seldom has a more grand effect of light been depicted than the magnificent sunshine on the mountains of a tropical clime... It literally floods the canvas with celestial fire, and beams with glory like a sublime psalm of light." Henry Tuckerman, "New York Artists" (1856), Kelly 50.

[8] "Let me stand with bare head and expanding chest upon one of Church's mountain-peaks, gazing over a billowy flood of hills; at my feet, torrents dashing, half-seen, through clouds; while from the rifted heavens the southern sunshine pours, like God's benediction upon my temples." Anonymous, "Pictures Canvassed" (1847), Kelly 50.

is descended from the Puritans of the seventeenth century. David Huntington, who even characterizes Church's work as "Puritan baroque," sees it as a form of art that Puritanism took two centuries to produce.[9]

Actually the iconic value of American nature is simply the other side of the traditional Protestant rejection of the representation of God. It suits the Calvinist idea that nature is the "theatre of God's glory." In an America that was heir to the Puritans, the representation of landscape was a substitute for the representation of God. Whatever their differences in matters of religion, Thomas Cole, Church and Emerson belonged to this same cultural tradition; for them, the wilderness was a pathway to the divine and landscape painting a form of celebration of it.[10]

Church's work, an anthology of the American sublime, is thus also a theology. To enumerate the forms of the sublime is to list Divinity's attributes: the power and the glory, the mystery and the universality. Such a conception of art makes the painter a prophet, as one of Church's contemporaries said: "Truly 'there is an evangel in art as well as books,' and Church is among the prophets."[11] By his role as an intermediary, but not as a mediator, between transcendence and the world of men, by his ability to represent the absolute, as opposed to the contingency of human life and history, Church asserts his prophetic aim. The prophet sees not so much the future as the absolute on which it is based. More than any other American painter, Church took on the mission of America's prophetic seer. This appears

---

[9] Huntington 177.

[10] Cole, for example, wrote: "Amid [those scenes of solitude] the consequent associations are of God the creator–they are his undefiled works, and the mind is cast into the contemplation of eternal things" (Cole 102). Emerson asked: "Is not the landscape, every glimpse of which hath a grandeur, a face of him [God]?" (Emerson 1983, 42.)

[11] "Church's Picture of The North," anonymous press clipping on Church's *The Icebergs,* Huntington 86.

particularly clearly in another of the paintings inspired by his travels in the Andes, *Cotopaxi*.[12]

By its size (1.22 m by 2.16 m) as well as its high view over vast uninhabited expanses, this painting evokes a world of continental dimensions, where we can pick out images of the sublime according to Edmund Burke: waterfalls, steep rock cliffs, volcanoes, contrasts of shadow and light. The landscape is bathed in a supernatural luminosity. Yet the tone is different from that of *Andes of Ecuador*, for it suggests a new theme belonging to wartime America. Although inspired by the sublimity of the Andes, this painting from 1862 also suggests the conflict that was ravaging the United States. It expresses the struggle between the forces of good and the forces of evil, symbolized by light (the sun) and darkness (the volcano) in an apocalyptic vision corresponding to the way many American Protestants saw the Civil War.[13] As in the Apocalypse of John, good ultimately will triumph over evil, a victory prefigured by the luminous cross traced on the lake's surface by the sun's rays–a symbol of Christ's second coming. Evoking the cosmic dimension of history, *Cotopaxi* is not so much a work of hope as of faith in a revival which will affirm the primacy of the absolute, a celebration of God's providential plan for the world. Church's God reveals himself theatrically, in an effusion of glory somewhat reminiscent of baroque art.[14]

Paintings like *Andes of Ecuador* and *Cotopaxi* define too a certain relationship between art and the spectator. Indeed Church's paintings seem to take the viewer outside time, suspending the world's clamor in the fascinated contemplation of a universe that affirms his faith in God and in America. Doubt had no place in Church's thinking, and even during the Civil

---

[12] Church, *Cotopaxi*, 1862. Detroit Institute of Art, Detroit, Michigan.

[13] For a discussion of the Protestant view, see Morehead.

[14] Huntington (177-78) sees a similarity between an oil sketch by Church (*Study of Sunrise,* circa 1855-1860, New York, Cooper-Hewitt Museum) and Bernini's *Ecstasy of St. Theresa* (1645-1652, Rome, Church of Santa Maria della Vittoria).

War his art maintained its affirmative power. Church is thus not only the painter of a triumphant and conquering America, but also of an America which finds in the unity of the cosmos an answer to the danger of being torn apart–as if nature's unity exorcised the threat of national disintegration. Standing face to face with divine transcendence thus offers man, that spectator trapped in the immanence of his destiny, a form of regeneration or redemption. Faith in the prophetic mission of the artist is reinforced by a faith in the powers of art which Church inherited from Cole[15]. The artist, convinced that art's power can transform the viewer's awareness, is confident in his redemptive mission.

God's Nation

If all nineteenth-century landscape painting seems divided between presenting nature as man's creation or as God's, it is clear that Church's paintings belong primarily to the second category. Indeed Church's work seems a veritable anthology of the American sublime, from the north to the south of the continents, from the icebergs of Labrador to the volcanoes of the Andes, and including the falls of *Niagara*, the arch of the *Natural Bridge, Virginia,* or the Maine forest of *Twilight in the Wilderness.*[16] From this point of view the closest literary equivalent of Church would have to be Walt Whitman rather than Thoreau.[17]

---

[15] Cole, 98-101

[16] *Niagara,* 1857, Corcoran Gallery, Washington, D.C.; *Natural Bridge, Virginia,* 1852, Bayley Museum, University of Virginia, Charlottesville; *Twilight in the Wilderness,* 1860, Cleveland Museum, Cleveland, Ohio.

[17] Whitman's joint celebration of the self and of America, his determination to enfold in his song the immensity and variety of the continent, his cosmic vision of the world, all make him another great interpreter of the American sublime. Like Church's paintings, Whitman's poems bring the reader to an analogous feeling of

Geographically, however, something big is missing that was highly significant in Church's time. Why did Church never paint the American West? Why did he never go there, great traveler though he was? Nothing, it seems, sheds any light on this question. I might venture that, having followed Humboldt to South America, Church may have decided to exploit this field alone, leaving the Western landscape market to a colleague who specialized in it, Albert Bierstadt, an artist working in a similar spirit.

This spirit was that of manifest destiny, a vision of American nature whose sublimity could symbolize and sanctify the undertaking of this nation which considered its mission to be the conquest of nature. So a painting like *Niagara,* by its movement, power and scope, perfectly symbolizes America as regenerative force and partakes of the myth of a New Adam. American nature, being primitive, is close to the origin of the world and therefore to the Creator, so whoever immerses himself in it, in a recurrent baptism, finds himself renewed.[18] Nothing better symbolizes America than the rainbow linking sky and earth, this assurance of a new beginning which renews for American man–that castaway from the old world–the promise made to Noah. Ultimately, it is because the world is very old, and thus proof against corruption, that it is also new, a new Eden, and that American man is there reborn. Thus provided with the mission of redeeming man and proclaiming the millennium, this regeneration will spread throughout the world through the expansion of the American nation. From this close relation between primitive nature and the world's origin stems the human interest in science, particularly geology, which allows us to read the original text of the American continents, and so penetrate the secrets of the Creation.

---

expansion and infinite openness and of confidence in America's mission.

[18] This link between wilderness and divinity, of biblical origin, appears very clearly in Cole's famous declaration that "the wilderness is YET a fitting place to speak of God" (Cole, 100).

Niagara made Church the most famous American painter of his day. While Niagara Falls had already been the subject of innumerable literary descriptions and artistic representations[19] (including one by Cole[20]), Church's painting seems to have grasped and communicated this symbol of American nature like no other. Giving a view of the falls which does not strictly correspond to any actual point, yet rendered with a gift of observation and an objectivity unknown until then, *Niagara* earned Ruskin's admiration.[21] Church, the true prophet-seer of America, discovered the formula which best expressed the sublimity of the site. The artist, God's servant, seems to have withdrawn after having lent his hand to a revelation of which he is only the interpreter.[22] We find here one of the characteristics of form noted in *Andes of Ecuador*, a break between the plane of the picture and the spectator, which dramatizes the intent of Church's vision. Besides the suggestion of transcendence already mentioned, it quite obviously contributes, in this case, to the viewer's illusion that he is placed at the very edge of the falls, that nothing human separates him from Niagara. Yet this abrupt

---

[19] See especially Nathaniel Hawthorne, "My Visit to Niagara" (Hawthorne 244-50) and Adamson, *Niagara*.

[20] Cole, *Distant View of Niagara Falls*, 1830, Art Institute of Chicago. This painting, quite different from Church's, reveals Cole's tormented soul rather than reflecting a prophetic vision of America.

[21] Church had many of Ruskin's works in his library in Olana. Of interest in this context, these included volumes of the 1852 and 1856 editions of *Modern Painters* (Huntington 189 n33).

[22] As an anonymous critic wrote of *The Icebergs*: "It seems to me the secret is in the artist's earnestness and modesty,–in the 'sublime representation of himself.' He seems to display the Lord's beauty, and not his own skill: his flowers bloom, ice shimmers, and waterfalls weave their rainbows, to the praise of nature, the glory of God,–not Church. There is no machinery visible, no rehearsal-work: no one observes how the paint is spread; you would as soon stretch out your hand to feel the texture of an angel's wing; you do not think of texture. It is a vision." (Huntington 190 n71). For a thorough consideration of this question, see Monfort.

closeness, this immediacy does not overwhelm the viewer. Church's spectacle of Niagara Falls, in its very sublimity, helps us to characterize this aspect of his vision more precisely.

Schematically, we can approach this vision through two fundamental texts–Burke's essay, *A Philosophical Inquiry into the Origin of Our Ideas of the Sublime and the Beautiful* (1757), and Immanuel Kant's *Critique of Judgment* (1790). Burke, in the empirical tradition of Locke, bases his analysis of the sublime on the viewer's sensory experience of objects that are inherently capable of producing the feeling of the sublime. The sublime object occupies the mind completely, so that the mind's activity is suspended by a feeling of terror which is central to the experience.[23] Burke's is thus a psychological analysis of the sublime from which any moral consideration is absent. From quite the opposite side, Kant, as a defender of rationalism and what he calls transcendental idealism,[24] gives precedence to mind, ahead of object and sensation, affirming that "the sublime should not be sought in the things of nature, but only in our ideas."[25] Still, Kant recognizes that, without being a property of objects, the sublime is produced by *some* objects, and he makes a distinction between a "mathematical sublime" (i.e., as to size) and a "dynamic sublime" (i.e., as to power). Beyond their differences, both seem to share the ability to separate man from the use of his senses and raise him to the idea of the infinite and the absolute.[26]

---

[23] "Indeed terror is in all cases whatsoever, either more openly or latently the ruling principle of the sublime" (Burke 58).

[24] Kant gives the following definition: "By the transcendental idealism of all phenomena, I mean the doctrine according to which we view them, as a whole, as simple representations, and not as things in themselves ..." (Kant 1980, 299).

[25] Kant 1982, 89.

[26] "Sublime is that which, by the mere fact that we can think it, shows a faculty of the soul which goes beyond all measure of the senses." (Kant 1982, 90).

A whole tradition of American art history has sought to connect two different esthetics to these two concepts of the sublime, the difference between the Burkean and the Kantian experience being typified in the difference between a theatrical sublime, in which majesty and terror are produced by the action and force of nature's elements, and a contemplative sublime, in which the internal feeling of perceiving space and time is the essential agent. In line with the first, the great tradition of romanticism would be, to give one example, Cole's painting, while the second would correspond to the so-called luminist movement, represented chiefly by Fitz Henry Lane, Martin Johnson Heade, Sanford Gifford and John Frederick Kensett. It remains then to locate Church among these contemporaries.

By his emphasis on the grandeur and power of American nature, and thus on exterior forms of nature which seem to be imposed upon men, Church seems to belong to the Burkean tradition of the sublime. Still, we must admit that the idea of danger or terror is absent from Church's art. Even in his most grandiose works, the spectator is not terrified or shaken, but magnetized, fascinated by the power of an apparent metaphysical drama. Church's grandiose visions are too serene, too heavily suffused with the feeling of a benevolent power to inspire terror. It is significant, for example, that the critic of *Andes of Ecuador* cited earlier speaks of "God's benediction" in this work.[27] Instead of crushing humanity, this sublimity calls forth in him the feeling of rising toward the infinite or absolute. The place that man occupies in the very heart of Church's paintings is further proof: though very small compared to the nature which surrounds them, the figures we see there are not creatures overwhelmed by the power that dominates them; they are gently enfolded by a nature with which they live in harmony, in the

---

[27] See note 8. Another part of this criticism quoted by Kelly (49) expresses very clearly this relationship of fascination between painter and spectator. We are closer here to that "magic power" of light that Asher B. Durand writes about in *Letters on Landscape Painting* (1855), Kelly 50.

paradoxical proximity of the divine. Still elsewhere–for example in *View of Cotopaxi*[28]–humans appear more exactly as witnesses to the manifestation of transcendence with whom the viewer is supposed to identify.

In sum, it would seem that Church's sublime is located closer to, yet is not identical to, Kant rather than to Burke, whose conception of the sublime could perhaps be defined as the absolute sense-experience.[29] For Church esthetics were part of a Protestant theology in which sensitivity as such always remained more or less suspect. The only thing that redeemed it was that it afforded intuition of the divine, and indeed Church's passion for science, as we shall see, also supported an approach to the world via the senses. For Church the sublime was an experience at once deeply sensual *and* supremely intellectual–a reconciliation between the senses and the mind that demonstrates, perhaps, the difference between the philosopher and the artist.[30]

Between Science and Theology

It is difficult for us, at a time when art has acquired its independence as an interpretation of the world, to accept a form of painting–that of Church or Cole–so laden with a meaning that lies beyond it. We have learned to do without a "backstage" to our reality, and nothing seems more remote from our sensitivity than a work of expression which always refers beyond itself. Cole believed it was the artist's double mission to present the world available to our senses and, through it, to evoke the human condition. Church, as a good disciple of Cole's, always remained faithful to this double concept of landscape painting. True, he

---

[28] 1857, Art Institute of Chicago.

[29] A deeper analysis of the Kantian sublime would show perhaps that for Kant the feeling of the sublime had more to do with man's grandeur–to the extent that man is thereby endowed with a "spiritual faculty" that is reason–than with God's.

[30] It should be noted that, significantly, Kant excluded art from his analysis of the sublime.

abandoned the allegorical manner characteristic of his master, but he continued to believe that painting had a moral and didactic vocation, which he simply restated in plainly scientific terms: art contributes to the decipherment of "the book of nature," in the prevalent expression of the time. Emerson notably evoked this idea in *Nature*:

> A life in harmony with nature, the love of truth
> and of virtue, will purge the eyes to understand
> her text. By degrees we may come to know the
> primitive sense of the permanent objects of
> nature, so that the world shall be to us an open
> book, and every form significant of its hidden
> life and final cause.[31]

The key to this new importance of science in Church's practice is, once again, his discovery of the writings of Humboldt, whom Church had begun to read around 1850-51, four or five years after the end of his apprenticeship period with Cole and two or three years after Cole's death. Humboldt's *Cosmos*, one chapter of which bears upon landscape painting and its links with science, profoundly inspired his practice as a painter. Humboldt expounded a conception of the world whose principal traits were its unity and harmony, and he called for a landscape art which could combine the sense of wonder before the beauty of nature with the rigor of scientific observation, reaffirming the didactic mission of art:

> ...and no doubt the sublime grandeur of creation
> would be better known and better felt, if in the
> big cities, near the museums, the public could
> freely view panoramas in which a sequence of
> scrolled paintings would represent landscapes
> seen from different degrees of longitude and

---

[31] Emerson 1983, 25.

latitude. By multiplying the means by which we help to present in interesting images the whole of natural phenomena, we can familiarize man with the unity of the world and make him feel more keenly nature's harmonious concert.[32]

Church found in Humboldt not only a conception of nature, and the confirmation of landscape painting's ability "to combine the visible and invisible in our contemplation of nature,"[33] but also a method (on-site sketching,)[34] the union of contemplation and thought,[35] the idea of a landscape as a synthesis of a region, and finally Humboldt's passion for the

---

[32] I quote from Humboldt 1860, v. 2, pt. 2, "Landscape Painting in its Influence on the Study of Nature," 82-98. (The traditional English translation by E. C. Otté went through more than a dozen editions from 1849 to 1899, and was reprinted in 1997 by Johns Hopkins Press. –Ed.)

[33] Humboldt 1860, 82. Humboldt remained discreet on the question of religion.

[34] "Colored sketches, taken directly from nature, are the only means by which the artist, on his return, may reproduce the character of distant regions in more elaborately finished pictures; and this object will be the more fully attained where the painter has, at the same time, drawn or painted directly from nature a large number of separate studies of the foliage of trees; of leafy, flowering, or fruit-bearing stems; of prostrate trunks, overgrown with Pothos and Orchideæ; of rocks and of portions of the shore, and the soil of the forest. The possession of such correctly-drawn and well-proportioned sketches will enable the artist to dispense with all the deceptive aid of hot-house forms and so-called botanical delineations" (94).

[35] "Landscape painting, though not simply an imitative art, has a more material origin and a more earthly limitation. It requires for its development a large number of various and direct impressions, which, when received from external contemplation, must be fertilized by the powers of the mind, in order to be given back to the senses of others as a free work of art. The grander style of heroic landscape painting is the combined result of a profound appreciation of nature and of this inward process of the mind" (94-95).

Andean land.[36] It was under Humboldt's influence that Church made two expeditions in the Andes in 1855 and 1857, which remained a major source of inspiration throughout his career. He identified himself to such an extent with Humboldt's vision that, proud of the success of *Heart of the Andes* in 1859, he wanted to send his work to Berlin so that the great man could view it. Unfortunately Humboldt, aged 90, died in the meantime.

Heart of the Andes corresponds perfectly to Humboldt's esthetic. First of all, it is a composite landscape which corresponds to no precise place. Nowhere in the Andes can you see, from the same point, the luxuriant vegetation of the lower grounds and the snow-covered peaks of the mountains: instead, Church reconstitutes an imaginary landscape intended to evoke the variety and unity of a whole part of the world–indeed of the entire world, if we assume that the very high mountain symbolizes the Arctic. With all his virtuosity, Church inscribes the greatest possible profusion of natural detail, particularly botanical, in his painting, which seems to portray the new Eden and which earned him, in spite of some critics, the admiration of the American public. *Heart of the Andes* thus became the supreme example of those great compositions intended to fascinate the spectator by synthesizing on the one hand a vast panoramic movement suggesting the infinitude of the world and the transcendence which animates it, and on the other hand, a

---

[36] Humboldt invites each of us to "feel what an inexhaustible treasure remains still unopened to the landscape painter between the tropics in both continents, ... and how all the spirited and admirable efforts already made in this portion of art fall far short of the magnitude of those riches of nature of which it may yet become possessed. Are we not justified in hoping that landscape painting will flourish with a new and hitherto unknown brilliancy when artists of merit shall more frequently pass the narrow limits of the Mediterranean, and when they shall be enabled, far in the interior of continents, in the humid mountain valleys of the tropical world, to seize, with the genuine freshness of a pure and youthful spirit, on the true image of the varied forms of nature?" (93).

painstaking attention to detail and scientific exactitude. In this way providing a visual equivalent of the Pascalian notion of the "two infinites,"[37] Church rapidly made a name for himself by his ability to portray, almost to infinity, the richness of the natural world. Church was the painter of transcendence, not of the supernatural, which is a world without substance. His sense of detail guarantees a materiality that evokes an always possible link with transcendence–as if such physicality affirmed the reign of Incarnation, a form of immanence suited to sustaining humanity's aspirations. His painting was not a consolation, but a promise. In this, Church differed from Cole, who was haunted by the fall of man, and put his faith more exclusively in an intimate reality beyond a physical world upon which he never gazed as passionately as Church did.

However, in a more immediate way, this precision of detail also had enchantment and instruction as its aim. For, in the words of Theodore Winthrop, a writer friend of Church's and the author of a brochure explaining *Heart of the Andes,* "a great work of art is a delight and a lesson."[38] One must note that, in this pictorial tradition where seeing involved knowing rather than perceiving, these paintings were made to be, not simply looked at, but looked at in detail. In the exhibition prospectuses announcing *Heart of the Andes*, people were requested to come with binoculars in order to be able to focus on one or another detail[39]. That could only reinforce the break with the viewer already mentioned, as if the spectator, leaving corporality behind to become pure sight, attained the promise of contact with transcendence. Faith in America is fused with faith in vision–regenerated humanity, the new Adam, has found sight again–and faith in the possibility of knowledge, especially scientific knowledge, which was then considered a means of access to the divine.

---

[37] Pascal, 21-28.
[38] *A Companion to* The Heart of the Andes (1859), Kelly and Carr, 31.
[39] Avery 35.

It was this synthesis of faith and knowledge that was challenged by Darwinism in 1859, the year of *The Origin of Species*. That watershed year marks the end of a world, at least symbolically, for it witnessed at the same time the publication of Darwin's book and the death of Humboldt.[40] Darwin's theory of evolution marked a considerable break with the dominant world-view–the more so in the United States, where its cataclysmic effect soon dovetailed with the catastrophe of the Civil War. After Darwin, nature–having become the domain of struggle and chance–seems to lead us away from God, not toward him. The idea of the design and metaphysical finality of the world–of Providence–crumbles. Perhaps this is one reason Church now turned toward the Old World–toward history and no longer toward nature, to pursue his quest of the divine. In 1867-1868, Church, like many artists and writers of the period,[41] undertook his Voyage to the Orient, to those places consecrated by history or the Bible which furnished the subject for numerous paintings in the following years.

Church and Thoreau: Two World Views

Even if, for several years beginning in 1872, Church returned to tropical landscapes–among them *Morning in the Tropics*,[42] considered his last "great painting"–these more intimist paintings have an elegiac tone. One can't help seeing in them a desire to get away from a historical time cruelly dissociated from all millennial promise by the Civil War, and from a natural world that the Darwinian revolution had deprived of its metaphysical dimension. As a whole Church's painting would continue to offer the optimistic vision of a deeply pre-Darwinian world, a world whose equilibrium was unshakable. Because this is a final resurgence of the ancient world, this

---

[40] See Gould's essay (Kelly 94-107).

[41] Herman Melville, for example, had made such a voyage in 1856-1857. (See Chapter 10.)

[42] 1877, National Gallery of Art, Washington DC.

painting can touch us–a world whose key ideas are unity, harmony, and the certainty of divine presence.

Thoreau, in contrast, although he is contemporaneous with Church and like him inhabits an almost entirely pre-Darwinian world, nevertheless seems to me to belong to a different order. Thoreau's world–that of his maturity in any case, in the 1850s–is, I believe, imprinted with a certain skepticism; it is a world of the finite, over whose fate God no longer clearly presides. While the idea of a world "behind" reality was disappearing, the world of infinitude could be saved only by a purely human enterprise–the work of vision, the patient exercise of a gaze too lucid not to be sensitive to the historical unfolding of secularization, and participating in it after a fashion, perhaps in spite of itself. The intensity of this divergence becomes evident on reading Thoreau's entire Journal, or perhaps more simply on reading *The Maine Woods*, whose three sections present a condensed image of Thoreau's intellectual adventure.[43]

In fact, if we had to establish a relationship between Thoreau and American painting of the mid-nineteenth century, perhaps it would be with Cole, whose religious convictions Thoreau certainly did not have, but with whom he shared a pessimistic temperament and a skepticism about the direction America was taking. Thus the whole of *The Maine Woods* can be read as an allegorical cycle in the manner of Cole, a sort of equivalent of Cole's famous *Course of Empire* (1834-1836). Although wild nature rather than "empire" lies at the heart of each of these three narratives, Thoreau's vision traces a progression analogous to Cole's four paintings, moving from a strictly wild state ("Ktaadn") to a final state of desolation ("The Allegash and East Branch"), by way of a pastoral state ("Ktaadn" and part of "Chesuncook")–preceding a phase of

---

[43] Part one, "Ktaadn," was first published in 1848. Part two, "Chesuncook," was composed partly in 1853-1854 and appeared in 1858. The third part, "The Allegash and East Branch," composed essentially in 1857-1858 and left unfinished, was first published in the posthumous three-part *The Maine Woods* (1864). (See Chapter 2.)

accomplishment (imaginary, certainly) and of destruction (quite real) in the remainder of "Chesuncook." Simplifying, one could say that Thoreau, like Cole, conceives America in an apocalyptic–cyclical– fashion,[44] whereas Church conceives it along a linear and progressive post-millenarism. In "The Allegash and East Branch" God has deserted the world, leaving only a fortuitous shadow hovering over it.[45] The pantheistic identity of God and nature has been replaced by a world where materiality prevails and where the future of feeling is more uncertain.

Let us return to Church's fascination with the forests of Maine by considering his *Twilight in the Wilderness*. Capturing the magic of a sunset in wild nature with the same brilliance as the spellbinding nature of Niagara Falls, Church reads in it all the mystery of a virgin continent sanctified by the divine. Beyond a vision darkened by shadows, cast perhaps by history (we are on the eve of the Civil War), the New World, theatre of an ultimate reconciliation of man and nature, appears with its radiant horizon as a promise of resurrection. Nothing, on the other hand, appears more distant from the heroic visions of Church than Thoreau's landscapes of the Maine woods, sullied by man and deserted by the divine. In spite of the nationalist shading of the idea of national parks which he formulates at the end of "Chesuncook," Thoreau is fundamentally a stranger to the mix of nationalism and evangelism at the heart of manifest destiny.[46]

---

[44] The idea of cyclic time is fundamental in Thoreau (movement of the seasons, keeping a journal, fascination for that annual apocalypse, the falling of the leaves...).

[45] See the famous passage on the phosphorescent wood *The Maine Woods* (Thoreau 1972, 179-82).

[46] In February 1853 Thoreau wrote to H. G. O. Blake: "The whole enterprise of this nation which is not an upward, but a westward one, toward Oregon, California, Japan, etc., is totally devoid of interest to me, whether performed on foot or by a Pacific railroad. It is not illustrated by a thought, it is not warmed by a sentiment, there is

United as these two artists are by the same passion for scientific objectivity, Thoreau and Church seem to be opposites on a number of points–one the practitioner of a religious painting steeped in faith, emotion and certainty, the other a seeker and questioner characterized by doubt and even skepticism. While Church's painting fiercely demands adherence, Thoreau's work imperiously demands reflection, yet imposes no direction upon it. Both belong to the order of preachers and insist on the exemplarity of their reasoning, but Thoreau, as a good individualist, preaches above all to his own chapel–a chapel which celebrates America only for its utopian value, chanting no hymns to its historic destiny. To Church's painting of transcendence and a triumphant, perhaps stifling, exteriority, Thoreau opposes a world sufficiently uncertain that an interiority is affirmed, a breath. In the end, perhaps, Thoreau could have said about Church what he said about Ruskin (who nevertheless did influence him deeply): "The love of Nature and fullest perception of the revelation which she is to man is not compatible with the belief in the particular revelation of the Bible which Ruskin entertains."[47]

In fact, in spite of his immense success, both popular and critical, Church very early had to face accusations of superficiality and sensationalism. As early as 1864, James Jackson Jarves, in *The Art Idea*, declared that with Church, "color is an Arabian Night's Entertainment, a pyrotechnic display, brilliantly enchanting on first view, but leaving no permanent satisfaction to the mind, as all things fail to do which delight more in astonishing than instructing. Church's pictures have no reserved power of suggestion, but expend their force in *coup-de-main* effects..."

---

nothing in it which one should lay down his life for, nor even his gloves. ... No, they may go their way to their manifest destiny which I trust is not mine" (Thoreau 1958, 296). For Thoreau, if there is to be a millennium, it can only be an inner one, as the next chapter discusses.

[47] Thoreau, Journal JX:147, October 29, 1857.

A few years later Henry James, after having seen *The Valley of Santa Ysabel*,[48] uttered these nicely murderous words: "As we looked at Mr. Church's velvety vistas and gem-like vegetation ... we felt honestly sorry that there was any necessity in this weary world for taking upon one's self to be a critic... Why not accept this lovely tropic scene as a very pretty picture, and have done with it?"[49] Granted, the canvas James viewed is not Church's finest. All the same, the contemporary viewer is left with the persistent impression that the richness of these images whose meaning is fixed is rather quickly exhausted. Church's images are so completely foreign to any feeling of instability that they petrify us and seem incapable of providing lasting nourishment. There is no evolution in Church's painting, because his world is not really one of experience but one of faith—the experience of the world seems to have no other function than to support or convey this faith. Quite the contrary, Thoreau's world is one of experience and intuition, not of belief and revelation. His prose does not arrest us with its dazzling splendor, but sets us in movement, draws us into the vertigo of a *being* of things which, though it is not the certain reflection of the divine, is for us all the more profound.

---

[48] 1875, Berkshire Museum, Pittsfield, Massachusetts.
[49] "On Some Pictures Lately Exhibited" (1875), Kelly 65.

2

Thoreau's "Chesuncook,"
or
Romantic Nature Imperiled:
An American Jeremiad

Although Thoreau scholarship has undergone profound change during the past two or three decades, critical reading of *The Maine Woods* usually remains framed within the once prevalent view of Thoreau's decline after *Walden*.[50] *The Maine Woods* comprises three different narratives or essays, composed over a period of a dozen years and revised during Thoreau's final illness. Each relates a trip that Thoreau made to the Maine woods: "Ktaadn" (1848) relates his 1846 trip, "Chesuncook" (1858) his 1853 trip,[51] and "The Allegash and East Branch" (published posthumously) his 1857 trip.[52] Thus, *The Maine Woods* is a trilogy, or a triptych. This has

---

[50] The most characteristic example of this critical approach is to be found in Adams and Ross. The authors bluntly declare that "the clearing of the Maine woods parallels [Thoreau's] own loss of imaginative power" (192).

[51] "Chesuncook" appeared in the June, July, and August 1858 issues of *The Atlantic Monthly.*

[52] There is evidence that Thoreau intended the three essays to form a single book; *The Maine Woods* as we know it was not published until 1864, two years after the author's death. For the history of the text, see Joseph J. Moldenhauer's "Textual Introduction" to *The Maine Woods* (Thoreau 1972), as well as his chapter entitled "*The Maine Woods*" in Myerson, 124-41 (esp. 130).

seldom been acknowledged by critics, who usually concentrate on "Ktaadn" and sometimes mention a few famous passages from the other two narratives, which otherwise do not meet the literary expectations of most readers.

In this essay I will focus on the book's second part. In "Chesuncook," the main theme of "Ktaadn"–man's historical or metaphysical relation to the wilderness–is taken up again and reworked or reinterpreted in a new light. From a structural point of view "Chesuncook" closely parallels "Ktaadn": the two narratives are about the same length, and comprise two main parts. The section from Thoreau's arrival to the moose-hunting scene broadly corresponds to the sense of excitement and heroism of much of "Ktaadn," while the pages immediately following the central moose hunt are characterized by a more reflective mood, leading to the famous coda supporting the view of nature as sanctuary. Like "Ktaadn," "Chesuncook" rests on a polarity between process and stasis, between man's physical intervention in nature and his spiritual involvement. But, beyond structural parallels between the two narratives, it seems that much has changed in Thoreau's relationship with nature.

An American Jeremiad: Thoreau as Preacher

In "Chesuncook," the wilderness is no longer a silent space conducive to meditation and introspection, but a stage for Thoreau's address to America, and this address characteristically takes the form of the jeremiad. Not only his famous self-definition as "chaplain to the hunters" (99),[53] but also his references to "the old Jesuit missionaries" (96; 104; 134-36), whose experience he seems anxious to relive and reincarnate, clearly indicate that he thinks of himself as a preacher in this

---

[53] Parenthetical page numbers in the text refer to Thoreau 1972 (paperbound reprints, 1983, 2004). For a detailed analysis of *The Maine Woods,* see my critical edition in French (Specq 2004).

essay. And when, after the moose killing, he starts lamenting the destruction of wilderness symbolized by the fate of trees and wild animals, one is vigorously reminded of that genre, the jeremiad, whose centrality to American thought has been demonstrated by Sacvan Bercovitch (1978). Bercovitch showed that the two-faceted American jeremiad was not only lamentation but also promise, and this fundamental structure is clearly visible in "Chesuncook," where Thoreau's lament over the destruction of wilderness prepares us for his final pro-conservation plea, which is rife with religious overtones.

Throughout "Chesuncook" Thoreau is eager to learn more about the moose and moose hunting–principally because of his ardent desire for knowledge of Indians and wild animals: "Though I had not come a-hunting, and felt some compunctions about accompanying the hunters, I wished to see a moose near at hand, and was not sorry to learn how the Indian managed to kill one" (99). I do not intend to deny the sincerity of his desire, but I would also suggest that Thoreau's need to stand witness to unspeakable acts and to report them (115-16) serves as a preparation for what he has to say. The rhetorical and expressionist qualities of the narrative and of Thoreau's subsequent thoughts (118-22) are used for their ultimately persuasive power.[54]

Thoreau's rhetoric of nature conservation in the coda to "Chesuncook" is prepared and sustained by the moose hunting story and its attendant reflections: Thoreau relies on a sentimental reaction to render his plea effective, in a way similar to Aldo Leopold. (In Leopold's *Sand County Almanac* the reader comes to realize that the "almanac" and "sketches" do not serve their own purpose, that they are not autonomous, but that they are subservient to Leopold's own preaching, which appears as their "upshot."[55]) Voicing a quest for purity

---

[54] See 137-39, for instance.

[55] *Sand County Almanac* (1949) is divided into three parts: "A Sand County Almanac" (Part I) and "Sketches Here and There" (Part II) mostly feature pieces of nature writing, while "The Upshot" (Part III)

and a desire for spiritual wholeness after his eager involvement in the moose hunting, Thoreau's sentimentalist speech[56] is meant to rally his audience and readership to his outraged denunciation of what he perceives as a desecration not only of nature but of man. The concluding paragraphs of "Chesuncook" (156), significantly, echo that denunciation through their emphasis on the conservation of nature as restoring man to himself and to his own dignity. The final questions demand a response from the reader to Thoreau's plea.

The breach of contract between man and nature forms the core of the apocalyptic theme in the last two narratives, in which Thoreau depicts a ground strewn with carcasses of moose or trees[57] and rages against a humanity engaged in a war against the wilderness.[58]

"Chesuncook" seems characterized by a change from the millenarian-type vision of "Ktaadn"–a linear and progressive conception of history–to an apocalyptic vision.[59] The theme is apocalyptic not only on account of Thoreau's iconography of destruction, but because Thoreau claims that war with the pines and the moose will lead to another relationship between man and nature: through its very excesses,

---

expounds the author's ecological ideas.

[56] "I already and for weeks afterward felt my nature the coarser for this part of my woodland experience, and was reminded that our life should be lived as tenderly and daintily as one would pluck a flower" (120).

[57] See for instance: "They had killed twenty-two moose within two months, but, as they could use very little of the meat, they left the carcasses on the ground" (135), or "you strip off its hide ..., cut a steak from its haunches, and leave the huge carcass to smell to heaven for you" (119). Similarly, both "Chesuncook" and "The Allegash and East Branch" contain numerous evocations of the Maine wilderness as a "mossy graveyard of trees" (236).

[58] "It is a war against the pines, the only real Aroostook or Penobscot war" (128).

[59] For this distinction see Miller, 107-36.

conquest of nature will bring out preservation of nature. In this sense there is nothing here but "a ruse of reason"–the fulfillment of America's particular relationship with nature through destruction.

From Jeremiad to Redemption: Nature as Sanctuary

For insight into Thoreau's rhetorical motivation, it is important to focus on the "coda," the last few paragraphs of "Chesuncook," in which he defines the idea of national parks. The meaning of this passage has been blurred by its importance in the history of environmental conservation, and by the popular image of Thoreau as a revolutionary who subverted the notion of "manifest destiny" by claiming that America's manifest destiny lay not in ever-increasing control over nature but in its conservation. Indeed, Thoreau has been rightly regarded as one of the first in a long line of thinkers eager to foster awareness of the dangers facing the Earth and to seek solutions for the future.[60] What is of interest to me here, however, is not the historical importance of Thoreau's proposal, but the process of thought which led him to advocate the idea of national parks.

First, I would like to outline the rhetorical structure of the coda. Thoreau tries to strike a balance between two apparently irreconcilable attitudes: defense of the wild and exaltation of a tamed, pastoral world–thus making us fully realize that our perception of nature is above all a cultural convention, a mental construction based on traditions proper to our own civilization. The coda may be divided into three parts. In the first part (151-55), predictably, Thoreau exalts the special character of wild nature and laments its destruction, in an eloquent speech whose tone and themes–freedom and slavery, economy, criticism of the Concord farmers, distrust of politics and religion–are reminiscent of *Walden,* and which is designed

---

[60] For Thoreau as pioneer conservationist, see Nash, 84-95 and 102-03; Dorman, 47-101.

to stir his audience and readership, as when he expostulates:

> And what are we coming to in our Middlesex
> towns? a bald, staring townhouse, or meeting-
> house, and a bare liberty-pole, as leafless as it is
> fruitless, for all I can see. We shall be obliged to
> import the timber for the last, hereafter, or splice
> such sticks as we have;–and our ideas of liberty
> are equally mean with these (154).

Or he is ironic about "model farms," which "are, commonly,
places merely where somebody is making money, it may be
counterfeiting. The virtue of making two blades of grass grow
where only one grew before does not begin to be superhuman"
(155). The most compelling line of this passage, however, is the
one where Thoreau resorts to very powerful apocalyptic imagery
to predict that if destruction of nature goes on "we shall be
reduced to gnaw the very crust of the earth for nutriment" (154).

It thus comes as a surprise to the reader when, at the
beginning of the second part (155-56), Thoreau suddenly turns
about to declare that "nevertheless, it was a relief to get back to
our smooth, but still varied landscape" (155). He asserts that "the
wilderness is simple, almost to barrenness" (155), and in an
image as powerful as that of the "crust of the earth," evokes the
fate of "a civilized man" in the wilderness, "who must at length
pine there, like a cultivated plant, which clasps its fibers about a
crude and undissolved mass of peat" (155). He then goes on to
extol pastoral landscapes as eloquently as he had praised wild
nature earlier, associating with them notions of "perfection" and
"true paradise," in a way reminiscent of the Paradise Regained
theme that is characteristic of millenarian faith:[61]

---

[61] See Novak, 4, 5: "If Wilderness became cultivated ..., it could still be
a Garden. If the Garden was not Paradise, it could offer the possibility
of a Paradise to be regained. To this idea of Paradise, original or
regained, much energy was devoted." The entire coda to

Perhaps our own woods and fields,–in the best
wooded towns, where we need not quarrel about
the huckleberries,–with the primitive swamps
scattered here and there in their midst, but not
prevailing over them, are the perfection of parks
and groves, gardens, arbors, paths, vistas, and
landscapes. They are the natural consequence of
what art and refinement we as a people have,–
the common which each village possesses, its
true paradise, in comparison with which all
elaborately and wilfully wealth-constructed
parks and gardens are paltry imitations. (155-56)

In this description of Concord as the *locus amoenus* of
the pastoral tradition, Thoreau clearly has in mind the landscapes
of England as perceived and interpreted through the language of
the picturesque, which he had become familiar with through his
devoted reading of William Gilpin.[62] The picturesque provided a
framework ensuring the perception of land as landscape, thus
granting the viewer a sense of familiarity with nature. Thoreau
emphasizes the character of the picturesque as a softer version of
the sublime in his remark about "the primitive swamps ... not
prevailing over" the other elements of the landscape. Strangely
enough, in the last two pages of "Chesuncook," England is
summoned to serve as a point of reference for Thoreau's view of

---

"Chesuncook" is a disquisition on this double figure of American
Paradise.

[62] See Richardson, 260-65: "Gilpin argued that 'roughness'
or 'ruggedness' 'forms the most essential point of difference between
the *beautiful* and the *picturesque*.' The beautiful is smooth, finished
and regular, while the picturesque is rough and irregular" (260).
Howarth (157) states that "in 'Chesuncook' Thoreau does not
acknowledge the limitations of subjectivity, and thus his vision of the
wilderness is appreciative and sentimental, schooled by his reading of
Gilpin rather than of Ruskin."

nature, both as embodiment of pastoral nature, and, in the last paragraph, as the forerunner of the idea of national preserves. Thoreau nevertheless remains fully American in his insistence on the democratic character of the American pastoral landscapes, which are not the product of aristocratic fancy but "the natural consequence of what art and refinement we as a people have," and of his proposed "national preserves," which would not be a product of the feudal system, but would reflect the values and genius of a people who "has renounced the king's authority," a people of freemen and not of "villains"[63] (156).[64]

With his proposal for the creation of national preserves, which forms the third and last part of the coda (156), Thoreau gives a further twist to his line of argument, and resolves the tensions between the two opposite poles of wild and tamed nature. The general idea is that portions of wilderness should be preserved because of wild nature's value as "a resource and a background, the raw material of all our civilization" (155), which man should resort to from time to time "for inspiration and [his] own true recreation" (156). Although this passage has been regarded as a formative text for the environmental movement, its emphasis is less on the intrinsic value of wilderness than on its necessity to civilization. Thoreau celebrates the virtues of a seesaw motion from one to the other—what he termed a "border life" in his

---

[63] The *Oxford English Dictionary* defines "villein" (or "villain") as "one of the class of serfs in the feudal system"; Thoreau chose the "villain" spelling to avail himself of the meaning of "villain" (and not "villein") as "a low-born, base-minded rustic; a man of ignoble ideas or instincts."

[64] Thoreau associates the wilderness with the feudal, and the pastoral with the aristocratic. This parallel between the transformation of nature and that of society is perfectly in keeping with the developmental theories of civilization prevailing at the time, and takes its full meaning when we remember the connection between wilderness and savage peoples, who, in the nineteenth-century view, were doomed to extinction as a consequence of the "progress of civilization."

essay "Walking."[65] After his Promethean ascent in "Ktaadn," which forms the bright side of his wilderness experience, Thoreau here takes the shape of another, darker hero, Antaeus, who derives strength from each contact with his primal mother earth.[66]

I would now like to comment on Thoreau's proposal in greater detail, with "Ktaadn" as a background, so as to show what appear to me as its ambiguities. Two new major elements appear in Thoreau's vision of nature in "Chesuncook": the decreasing power of esthetic theories to endow wilderness with meaning, and a strong sense of nostalgia.

In the first place, Thoreau's account, as opposed to "Ktaadn," testifies to his difficulty in perceiving wild land as landscape. The entire paragraph beginning "Nevertheless, it was a relief to get back to our smooth, but still varied landscape" (155) shows that he can no longer fully comprehend the wilderness in esthetic terms, as though the language of the picturesque and the sublime had become ineffective. We can see the extent of this change if we hark back to a passage from the beginning of "Ktaadn" where Thoreau describes the sawmills at Oldtown:

> Through this steel riddle, more or less coarse, is
> the arrowy Maine forest, from Ktaadn and

---

[65] Thoreau 1980a, 130. "Walking" was given as a lecture in 1851-1852, and again in 1856-1857. Contrary to Adams and Ross, who claim that the coda to "Chesuncook" (perhaps written in 1858 and not in 1853) shows "Thoreau moving away from the extreme celebration of the wild he expressed in 'Walking' and *Walden*" (199-200), I would argue that, in this respect, Thoreau's stance is perfectly consistent throughout these different texts.

[66] In Greek mythology Antaeus was a giant, the son of Earth, who gained renewed strength every time he was struck to the ground. Hercules, en route to his final labor to fetch the golden apples of the Hesperides, encountered Antaeus and finally choked him to death by hoisting him on his shoulders. Thoreau compares himself to Antaeus in *Walden* (Thoreau 1971, 155).

Chesuncook, and the head waters of the St. John, relentlessly sifted, till it comes out boards, clapboards, laths and shingles such as the wind can take, still perchance to be slit and slit again, till men get a size that will suit. Think how stood the white-pine tree on the shore of Chesuncook, its branches soughing with the four winds, and every individual needle trembling in the sunlight–think how it stands with it now–sold, perchance to the New England Friction Match Company! (5)

Although this passage from "Ktaadn" refers to the same "war against the pines" (128) as "Chesuncook," it clearly shows the healing power of esthetic discourse. At this stage Thoreau's sense of destruction is still easily overcome through an esthetically governed wishful thinking, and it does not lead to any idea of measures to be taken to preserve the wilderness. In the second narrative, however, a darker view of nature prevails, one which is increasingly interpreted in moral terms, since wilderness has come to be associated more often than not with confinement rather than freedom,[67] and to be seen as a place for wild behavior rather than spiritual regeneration. The ambivalence with which Thoreau invests the wilderness in the second part of *The Maine Woods* attests to his irregular relationship to the Puritan tradition.[68] In this respect, creating a national park would appear as a means of endowing wild nature with meaning. If landscape esthetics can no longer ensure its

---

[67] The same ambiguity prevails in the third narrative, "The Allegash and East Branch," where, toward the beginning, Thoreau states: "[we] were suddenly naturalized there and presented with the freedom of the lakes and the woods" (165), later to declare: "It is an agreeable change to cross a lake, after you have been shut up in the woods. ... To look down, in this case, over eighteen miles of water, was liberating and civilizing even" (197-98).

[68] See Nash, 23-43.

assimilation by the individual, then something else must take its place if nature is to remain meaningful. My contention is that, faced with a crisis of esthetic interpretive schemes, Thoreau here relied on ethics to support his search for meaning, and that in "Chesuncook" the moral sublime is substituted for the aesthetic sublime of "Ktaadn."

The second aspect is nostalgia. The whole passage is imbued with a sense of lost harmony between man and nature, whether wild or pastoral. He concludes his eulogy of the Concord landscape on the remark that "such were our groves twenty years ago" (156), and the coda's last paragraph particularly relies on the nostalgic image of a fantasized American natural paradise peopled with bear, panthers and Indians. The nostalgic desire for a reality supposed to be outside of historical time and authentic–nature or "primitive societies" in particular–has been shown to be a characteristic aspect of the tourist experience.[69] It is only appropriate that it should appear in a travel book avowedly intended for "future tourists" which is an attempt at promoting the creation of public spaces (which today are among the world's major tourist attractions). Even if it is true that Thoreau, when he puns on the two meanings of the word "recreation" (156), dismisses the idea of recreation as "leisure," which he associates with idleness, he was nevertheless a tourist, and defines himself elsewhere as a "traveler in the forest." According to Dean MacCannell, all tourists pursue a quest for authenticity which is a latter-day version of the universal need for the sacred and transforms the tourist into a kind of pilgrim. Through its designation as a national preserve, nature thus becomes a sacred object of the tourist ritual. In this respect, Thoreau's coda appears as an attempt to re-sacralize a nature desecrated by man's productive activities, and to ensure the possibility of future experiences of the sacred such as the one described in the mountain-top passage of "Ktaadn." "Chesuncook" shows Thoreau striving to save the very

---

[69] MacCannell, ch. 4.

possibility of transcendence, even as he makes it dependent upon man's will–in a gesture which we may regard as a final desperate burst of Romanticism.

Thoreau's proposal attempts to preserve by a pessimistic and nostalgic gesture a portion of wild nature, cut off as if by a bell jar from its real physical and historical environment, which is supposed corrupt–as if man were again to be admitted, if only temporarily, into the immovable reality of the Garden of Eden. The desire for Paradise was a salient feature of nineteenth-century American concern about the diminishing wilderness. "Chesuncook" embodies the common dream of escape from a fallen world and reintegration into the Garden of Eden, but Thoreau's originality is his split version of the Garden of Eden, which, integrating both the pastoral realm and the wilderness, partakes of both Arcadia and Utopia. In this sense Thoreau's idea is quintessentially American. Indeed, one may see the national park as standing for the nation's purity–as a place symbolizing America's eternally regenerative powers. The national park is thus not only a cultural icon, reflecting the New World's need for monuments, but a metonymy for the nation. This is a considerable rhetorical change from the metaphorical vision of the mountaintop in "Ktaadn"–in which nature appeared as the projective scene of man's psychic experience of the world.

Yet it should not blind us to the deep continuity between Thoreau's two narratives. In "Ktaadn" Thoreau achieved the domestication of the wilderness through the familiarizing power of estheticizing devices. In the same way, Thoreau's proposal for the creation of national parks enshrines the sublime, which is yet another way of domesticating it; and, while the end of "Chesuncook" claims an alternative usage of nature, it simultaneously asserts the irrelevance of nature outside of human presence. In fact, in some respects, "Chesuncook" pursues Thoreau's subscription to a progressive vision of history: if he expresses a desire to free nature from the limits of purely utilitarian constraints, and has relinquished the millenarian-type expectations of "Ktaadn," he still retains some faith in the march of American history, which alone ensures the civilizing of nature necessary to everyday life, and he puts forth a proposal that may justify the continuing reign of manifest destiny everywhere outside of the national parks. In other words, Thoreau here does not so much question the general relevance of the idea of a linear progression of history, and of a vision where future and progress coincide, as he offers adjustments to the notion of manifest destiny, its reshaping within a different framework.

Nevertheless, Thoreau's effort to restore the wilderness to its value as territory not of alienation and destruction but of personal and national promise stops short of identification with the popular doctrine of manifest destiny: precisely, Thoreau refuses to identify personal with national regeneration. National action is no substitute for continuing self-reform, and the fact remains that, for Thoreau, if the idea of millennium is retained, its advent and fulfillment can only be an internal experience, which means that millennium is neither within collective historical time (post-millenarism) nor beyond history (pre-millenarism), but in the recesses of the individual's spiritual life.

3

Thoreau's Flowering of Facts and the Truth of Experience

Your greatest success will be simply to perceive that such things are...
—Thoreau, Journal, Oct. 4, 1850

In an essay written at Emerson's prompting and published in 1842, entitled "Natural History of Massachusetts," Thoreau concluded: "Let us not underrate the value of a fact; it will one day flower in a truth."[70] This statement is characteristic of the early years of Thoreau's career, when his approach to reality was by and large framed within Emerson's theory of correspondences. This theory, which Emerson expounded in his book *Nature* (1836), postulated the existence of a relationship between natural "facts" and spiritual "truths," the world being "a remoter and inferior incarnation of God."[71] Emerson thus adhered to the Neo-Platonist faith in an ultimate and transcendent order of reality or beauty toward which everything intuitively aspires–an idea suggested by the organic metaphor of "flowering." Perceptions of the natural world thus pointed–teleologically and theologically–toward a supreme reality, and the sense of human existence, as defined by Emerson in his essays, was to achieve unity with that higher order through a release of one's creative powers, whose symbol and model was the poet:

---

[70] Thoreau 2002, 22.
[71] Emerson 2001, 50.

... the poet turns the world to glass, and shows us
all things in their right series and procession.
For, through that better perception, he stands one
step nearer to things, and sees the flowing or
metamorphosis; perceives that thought is
multiform; that within the form of every creature
is a force impelling it to ascend into a higher
form...[72]

Emerson's conception of the world implied that facts
should be decoded and redeemed through generalization and
spiritualization, as opposed to their individual statement–in order
to become truly meaningful. What was to be reached through
this assumption of facts into higher meaning he indifferently
called science or philosophy.

In this perspective the enjoyment of nature advocated by
Emerson was merely a preparatory step toward the appreciation
of the superior reality of the spirit. Emerson never abandoned the
material universe, but he was prone to leave aside the immediate
aspects of reality to express the forces which animate the world,
the circuits of energy and spirit, the power of thought which
"dissolves the material universe, by carrying the mind up into a
sphere where all is plastic."[73] This dissolution especially affected
one's experience of time and space: "Man is greater..., and the
universe less, because Time and Space relations vanish as laws
are known" (40). Emerson thus developed a metaphysical vision
at the expense of the physical world, perceived as "a dream and a
shade" (47). His approach to the world appears to be tinged with
a Puritan distrust of physicalness, and more particularly with the
heritage of the Puritan typological reading of reality, in which
facts were transformed into religious statements.[74]

---

[72] "The Poet," Emerson 2001, 189-90.
[73] "Fate," 270. The next two parenthetical page references are also
to Emerson 2001 (*Emerson's Prose and Poetry*).
[74] Emerson's theory of correspondences reflected a deep distrust of
the material reality of things, as recognized by his contemporaries.

In his early years, when he was most influenced by Emerson, Thoreau likewise believed "that there is an ideal or real nature, infinitely more perfect than the actual as there is an ideal life of man,[75] thus asserting the identity of the "ideal" and the "real" in typically Platonist fashion. Correlatively, Thoreau also believed that man's relation to the natural world depended upon the search for a bridge between the physical and the metaphysical so as to achieve a higher level of self-realization:

> In purer more intellectual moods we translate our gross experiences into fine moralities. ...The laws of nature are science but in an enlightened moment they are morality and modes of divine life. In a medium intellectual state they are esthetics.[76]

For instance Margaret Fuller confided in her Journal in 1842: Emerson "does not care for facts, except so far as the immortal essence can be distilled from them. He has little sympathy with mere life: does not seem to see the plants grow, merely that he may rejoice in their energy." (Rosenwald 90). And Nathaniel Hawthorne noted in 1842 also: "Mr. Emerson is a great searcher for facts, but they seem to melt away and become insubstantial in his grasp" (Koster 41). One may thus understand why Emerson, in a letter to Fuller, confessed his disappointment at Thoreau's "*Natural History of Massachusetts*," which contained the seeds of the truth of the later Journal. One may find an even more direct illustration of Emerson's distrust of facticity in a letter of May 6, 1843 to his brother William, in which he remarked of Thoreau that "he is a bold & a profound thinker though he may easily chance to pester you with some accidental crotchets and perhaps a village exaggeration of the value of facts" (*Norton* 1162).

[75] J1:481; Nov. 2, 1843. Throughout this book, references to the preferred (but stll incomplete) "Princeton" edition of Thoreau's multivolume Journal use Arabic numerals (e.g., J1); references to the Torrey-Allen edition use Roman numerals (e.g., JXIV).

[76] J1:468; Sept. 28, 1843.

And in *A Week on the Concord and Merrimack Rivers,* he defined the "material universe" as "but the outward and visible type" of the immaterial,[77] thus directly echoing the language of typology, which was itself an adaptation of Platonism by New England Puritans.

As a consequence, the young Thoreau was inclined to dissolve the material component of the transcendental by establishing an analogical relation to the world of spirit, as exemplified by such statements as the following:

> I learned to-day that my ornithology had done me no service— The birds I heard, which fortunately did not come within the scope of my science–sung as freshly as if it had been the first morning of creation, and had for background to their song an untrodden wilderness–stretching through many a Carolina and Mexico of the soul.[78]

These lines also show how Thoreau strove to achieve transcendence by condensing into some essential reality the multiple aspects presented by things.

The overall result of the Emersonian theory of correspondences was to transform the material actuality of experience into the equivalent of an inner or superior reality. Through a metaphysical leap from the particular into a universalized form of abstraction, transcendentalism involved a transcendence not only of materiality (or substance) but also of temporality (or situatedness): the poet "poetizes, when he takes a fact out of nature into spirit – – He speaks without reference to time or place."[79] The writer's achievement, in this perspective, was to glimpse the immutable and intangible that underlie the empirical world.

---

[77] Thoreau 1980b, 386.
[78] J1:115; Mar. 4, 1840.
[79] J1:69; Mar. 3, 1839.

Beyond Emersonianism

I would now like to outline Thoreau's move beyond Emersonianism in the 1850s, and more particularly to suggest how Thoreau's later Journal reflects his evolution towards a relation to the world which runs counter to the depreciation of experience, materiality, and temporality that I have delineated.

In fact, even during the 1840s, Thoreau's writings were more complex than my brief presentation has suggested. They manifested a self-conflicted character (especially in *A Week on the Concord and Merrimack Rivers)*, alternately celebrating the value of facts or their transcendentalization. That divided vision gave way to a markedly different world view in the 1850s. Although the change in Thoreau's approach both to the natural world and to the nature of his journalizing was gradual, the major turning point occurred between 1849 and 1851, when he embarked on the dedicated study and recording of nature in his pages. A crucial aspect of that change was the transformation of the Journal from a writer's repository of ideas for future works to an increasingly autonomous undertaking:

> I do not know but thoughts written down thus in a journal might be printed in the same form with greater advantage–than if the related ones were brought together into separate essays. They are now allied to life–& are seen by the reader not to be far fetched– It is more simple– less artful–I feel that in the other case I should have no proper frame for my sketches. Mere facts & names & dates communicate more than we suspect–Whether the flower looks better in the nosegay–than in the meadow where it grew–&

we had to wet our feet to get it! Is the scholastic
air any advantage?[80]

Beginning in late 1850, Thoreau's Journal became much more regular, with systematically dated entries. It eventually came to fill 14 volumes and more than 7,000 pages in the first full printed edition.[81] If there ever was a place where Thoreau managed "to speak... *without* bounds,[82] it was in his *"extravagant"* Journal, which bears witness to the intensity and seriousness of his involvement with nature–indeed, to his achieving the "heroic life [he] had dreamed of."[83] As a literary project, the Journal ceased to be subservient to separate literary ends–no longer cannibalized for other works, it became instead a tool for perceiving and relating to the world.

This new function derived from the fact that Thoreau's approach to the natural world simultaneously underwent a deep transformation–partly, as Laura Dassow Walls has shown, as a result of reading Alexander von Humboldt's works in 1850.[84] What Thoreau came to reject was the metaphysics of transcendentalism, not its moral or ethical intent. He departed from a world-view in which phenomenal nature functions as a transparent symbol opening on to the supreme reality of the

---

[80] J4:296; Jan. 27, 1852.

[81] For an analysis of the transformation of Thoreau's Journal in the early 1850s, see Cameron, as well as the Historical Introductions to J3 and J4.

[82] *Walden,* Thoreau 1971, 324.

[83] J2:242, written about April 1846. Walls interprets Thoreau's increasing passion for nature as a substitute for human friendships and a sublimation of "desire" (123). 1 believe that, beyond the role played by psychological forces, the poet's craving for the world was more "metaphysical," or rather "ontological," even as it was deeply experiential. What gives particular value and power to Thoreau's endeavor is that it is not limited to the statement of philosophical principles, but embodied in an existential project of the utmost intensity.

[84] Walls, esp. 134-47.

ideal. Idealism's sense of man's alienation in the material world, in particular, proved impossible for Thoreau to reconcile with his growing engagement with nature. Increasingly during the 1850s, experience no longer seemed subject to the unfolding of a divinely ordained universe in which facts were merely subservient to spiritual truths. Instead, experience now became a complex response to a more undetermined world in which the perceiver plays an essential part.[85]

The Truth of Experience

While in Emerson's view experience pointed toward a revelation of the underlying–or overarching–metaphysical unity of the world, and while art functioned as a manifestation of esthetic and spiritual truth, Thoreau insisted on the intrinsic value of experience: the entry of January 27, 1852 quoted above is thus an explicit recognition of the primacy of experiential facts. In other words, "truth" was no longer to be reached beyond one's experience of the world, but within that experience itself. Experience thus no longer meant alienation but rather joy and liberation (if occasionally tempered by anxiety about the daunting massiveness of reality):

> Men esteem truth remote, in the outskirts of the
> system, behind the farthest star, before Adam
> and after the last man. In eternity there is indeed
> something true and sublime. But all these times
> and places and occasions are now and here. God
> himself culminates in the present moment, and
> will never be more divine in the lapse of all the

---

[85] It must be emphasized that this transition was gradual. In 1852, for instance, Thoreau could still marvel at the discovery that "the year... is a circle" and that "every incident is a parable of the great teacher" (J4:468; Apr. 18, 1852). Indeed, he may never have abandoned his faith in some sort of divine immanence in the world, although he certainly qualified it as time went on.

ages. And we are enabled to apprehend at all
what is sublime and noble only by the perpetual
instilling and drenching of the reality which
surrounds us.[86]

Thoreau thus eloquently pleaded for the situatedness of
all knowledge and significance, as well as for the total
engagement required of anyone eager to enjoy an authentically
poetic relation to the world.[87] The later Journal reverses the
sense of ascesis, as though reaching truth no longer was at the
expense of physical density, or substance, but rather required one
to engage ever more deeply with the litanies of the visible and
the tangible. As he craved for "a perpetual instilling and
drenching of the reality which surround[ed]" him, Thoreau was
not after a higher reality, but a deeper reality– "Let deep answer
to deep."[88] The higher plane to be reached thus was not that of
the ideal or the symbolic, but that of coexistence in time, a form
of reciprocity or exchange between nature and the observer.
Thoreau grew skeptical of the redemptive promise of the eternity
of the symbol, but he believed in the redemptive value of true
acts of perception:

Your greatest success will be simply to perceive
that such things are ...; if it is required that you
be affected by ferns, that they amount to
anything, signify anything, to you, that they be
another sacred scripture and revelation to you,
helping to redeem your life, this end is not so
surely accomplished.[89]

In this passage deeply imbued with religious vocabulary,
Thoreau makes meaning primarily personal: through his

[86] *Walden,* Thoreau 1971, 96-97.
[87] For a further discussion of this "poetic condition," see Specq 1995.
[88] J8:176; June 5, 1854.
[89] JXII:371-72; Oct. 4, 1859.

requirement that things "signify [something] *to you,*" that they be "another ... revelation *to you*" (my emphasis), he substitutes personal significance for pre-determined theological interpretations as the only valid criterion for assessing the value (or "success") of experience. Thoreau's suggestion of the redemptive power of the individual's attention to the material world counters the modern tendency of humankind to cut itself off from the physical world, thus providing the rationale for his environmental thought, notably his conception of man's place in nature as defined in "Chesuncook," the second part of *The Maine Woods*.

The supreme achievement is to be of the world, not against it, and this, Thoreau insisted, is an act of love: "My Journal should be the record of my love. I would write in it only of the things I love. My affection for any aspect of the world."[90] The primacy of "Love" is essential as it distinguishes Thoreau's quest for significant experience from a mere search for meaning. Indeed Thoreau kept insisting on a relation to the world that was not merely intellectual, but intensely sensuous, providing what William James called "the richest intimacy with facts"[91]:

> I begin to see such an object when I cease to *understand* it–and see that I did not realize or appreciate it before–[92]

> A fact stated barely is dry. It must be the vehicle of some humanity in order to interest us ... It must be warm, moist, incarnated, have been breathed on at least. A man has not seen a thing who has not felt it.[93]

---

[90] J3:143; Nov. 16, 1850.
[91] James 13.
[92] J3:148; Nov. 21, 1850.
[93] JXIII:160; Feb. 23, 1860.

Thoreau's reference to the dryness of facts here no longer serves to justify their redemption through their spiritualization, but rather acts as a foil to his advocacy of a deeply sensuous relationship with nature that was rejected by religious and scientific thought alike. He dismisses both traditional religio-philosophical disdain for physical nature and modern science's vacuous blend of empiricism and rationalism.

One of the deepest of Thoreau's insights was his recognition that a perfect state of awareness could only be achieved through striking a balance–or more exactly living "a border life"[94]–between knowledge and ignorance. Throughout the 1850s, Thoreau entered in his Journal reflections on the necessity of alternately learning how to know, and how not to know, as exemplified by these two entries:

> How much of beauty–of color, as well as form–
> on which our eyes daily rest goes unperceived
> by us! No one but a botanist is likely to
> distinguish nicely the different shades of green
> with which the open surface of the earth is
> clothed,–not even a landscape-painter if he does
> not know the species of sedges and grasses
> which paint it. With respect to the color of grass,
> most of those even who attend peculiarly to the
> aspects of Nature only observe that it is more or
> less dark or light, green or brown. or velvety,
> fresh or parched, etc. But if you are studying
> grasses you look for another and different
> beauty, and you find it, in the wonderful variety
> of color, etc., presented by the various species.[95]

> It is only when we forget all our learning that we
> begin to know. I do not get nearer by a hair's
> breadth to any natural object so long as I

---

[94] "Walking," Thoreau 2002, 173.
[95] JXIV:3; Aug. 1, 1860.

presume that I have an introduction to it from some learned man. To conceive of it with a total apprehension I must for the thousandth time approach it as something totally strange. If you would make acquaintance with the ferns you must forget your botany. You must get rid of what is commonly called *knowledge of* them. Not a single scientific term or distinction is the least to the purpose, for you would fain perceive something, and you must approach the object totally unprejudiced. You must be aware that *no thing* is what you have taken it to be. In what book is this world and its beauty described? Who has plotted the steps toward the discovery of beauty? You have got to be in a different state from common. Your greatest success will be simply to perceive that such things are...[96]

For Thoreau scientific knowledge was both necessary and dangerous, an idea summarized in his statement that "We hear and apprehend only what we already half know."[97] The essential word is "half," as opposed to complete ignorance, which prevents from perceiving, and to full "knowledge" of the idealist or scientific type, which precludes any true knowledge, as it tends to substitute what it "knows" for the direct encounter with the thing itself. If you don't know, you won't see; but if you know, you tend to substitute knowledge for experience: hence "Learn science and then forget it,"[98] a process which paves the way for "a true sauntering of the eye."[99] Truth lies not in a misguided faithfulness to appearances reduced to a dead set of visible properties, but in perpetually renewed experience, in the fluidity of knowledge:

---

[96] JXII:371; Oct. 4, 1859.

[97] JXIII:77; Jan. 5, 1860.

[98] J4:483; Apr. 22, 1852.

[99] J5:344; Sept. 13, 1852.

> I do not know that knowledge amounts to anything more definite than a novel & grand surprise or a sudden revelation of the insufficiency of all that we had called knowledge before. An indefinite sence [sic] of the grandeur & glory of the Universe. It is the lighting up of the mist by the sun.[100]

Thoreau's commitment to daily observation is thus elevated to a faith, and his celebration of the unsteadiness of knowing defines his approach to nature as a deeply religious–even mystical–experience. The Journal, simultaneously taking the "book of nature" and its religious substratum as a model and as a foil, makes it clear that there is no pre-existing text to be deciphered, even as it offers its own version of such a book.[101]

Thoreau's engagement with the natural world aimed to explore the inner workings of consciousness–what he called "the mysterious relation between myself & these things."[102] He insisted on the observer's ever-shifting relation with the external world, and on the centrality of the process of perceiving to the emergence of "reality":

> There is no such thing as pure *objective* observation. Your observation, to be interesting, *i.e.* to be significant, must be *subjective*. The sum of what the writer of whatever class has to report is simply some human experience, whether he be poet or philosopher or man of science. The man of most science is the man most alive, whose life is the greatest event.[103]

---

[100] J3:198; Feb. 27, 1851.
[101] For an analysis of the history and meaning of the idea of the book of nature, see St. Armand 1997.
[102] J4:468; Apr. 18, 1852.
[103] J8:98; May 6, 1854.

Committed to a process of world-making "by the interaction–the 'dance'–of the creative self and the world,"[104] Thoreau repeatedly made clear the importance of the "intention of the eye"[105] in the construction of reality–the essential part played by the observer in the creation of the reality that he sees and *inhabits*. Thoreau's *ethos* was inseparable from his concern with *oikos,* or our dwelling-place, and this is where his epistemology and his environmental advocacy intersect. He must have felt uncomfortable with the support which the dematerialization of nature ultimately lent to the enterprises bent on subjecting it. The subjugation of "facts" to the empire of thought may indeed appear as a mere justification of the claim of the "kingdom of man over nature," as Emerson called it.[106]

Based on a recognition that there is thus no objective, rational, stable image of the world that one may cling to or strive for, Thoreau's Journal invites us to a dizzying, unsettling encounter with the sheer enormity of the universe, restored to its full substance and temporality. Thoreau resisted idealism because it works toward the clarification of boundaries, and thus entails the transparency or dissolution of the material world. What he clearly relished was the gravitational pull of substance.

Substance versus Shadows

If the subservience of facts to a supreme order of reality drains them of any vitality and density of their own, Thoreau's Journal, on the contrary, displays a wonderful sense of physicality and situatedness–embodying Thoreau's dictum that "the constant endeavor should be to get nearer and nearer *here.*"[107]

---

[104] Peck 1990, 123.
[105] JXI:153; Sept. 9, 1858.
[106] *Nature*, Emerson 2001, 55.
[107] JXI:275; Nov. 1, 1858.

Imbued with an almost Darwinian sense of the priority of specifics over essences,[108] Thoreau felt more and more drawn toward a full engagement with compelling physical presences – as opposed to a theological essentialism for which essences exist in a superior or divine order of reality. Indeed, for Emerson–whose world was still fundamentally pre-Darwinian, as Lee Rust Brown has made clear in *The Emerson Museum*–"substance" was on the side of God, while nature appeared as the "scoriae of the substantial thoughts of the Creator."[109] And if Emerson repeatedly emphasized "transparency" as the unveiling of the supreme reality of the world, Thoreau delighted in the luminous opacity of "facts." Thoreau's sense of nature as substance prevails throughout the Journal of the 1850s, whether in botanical descriptions, for instance, or more elaborate scenes which may be less easily excerpted. The following extended passage from the entry of January 27, 1860 provides an example of such descriptions:

> Now I see, as I am on the ice by Hubbard's meadow, some wisps of vapor in the west and southwest advancing. They are of a fine, white, thready grain, curved like skates at the end. Have we not more finely divided clouds in winter than in summer? flame-shaped, asbestos-like? I doubt if the clouds show as fine a grain in warm weather. They are wrung dry now. They are not expanded but contracted, like spiculae. What hieroglyphics in the winter sky!

---

[108] In his journal for Mar. 8, 1860–just after his reading of Darwin's *Origin of Species* (first published in London, Nov. 24, 1859)–Thoreau emphasizes that *"nature* is a *becoming"* (JXIII:183). Walls notes that "even before the publication of *Origin of Species,* Thoreau was working along lines that can only be described as Darwinian" (189). The Darwinian revolution notably implied forms of reasoning based on the notion of populations rather than essences.

[109] Emerson 2001, 38-39.

Those wisps in the west advanced and increased like white flames with curving tongues,–like an aurora by day. Now I see a few hard and distinct ripple-marks at right angles with them, or parallel with the horizon, the lines indicating the ridges of the ripple-marks. These are like the abdominal plates of a snake. This occupies only a very small space in the sky. Looking right up overhead, I see some gauzy cloud-stuff there, so thin as to be grayish,– brain-like, finely reticulated; so thin yet so firmly drawn, membranous. These, methinks, are always seen overhead only. Now, underneath the flamy asbestos part, I detect an almost imperceptible rippling in a thin tower vapor,– an incipient mackerelling (in *form*). Now, nearly to the zenith, I see, not a mackerel sky, but blue and thin, blue-white, finely mixed, like fleece finely picked and even strewn over a blue ground. The white is in small roundish flocks. In a mackerel sky there is a parallelism of oblongish scales. This is so remote as to appear stationary, while a lower vapor is rapidly moving eastward.

Such clouds as the above are the very thin advance-guard of the cloud behind. It soon comes on more densely from the northwest, and darkens all.

No bright sunset to-night.

What fine and pure reds we see in the sunset sky! Yet earth is not ransacked for dye-stuffs. It is all accomplished by the sunlight on vapor at the right angle, and the sunset sky is constant if

you are at the right angle. The sunset sky is
sometimes more northerly, sometimes more
southerly. I saw one the other day occupying
only the south horizon, but very fine, and
reaching more than half-way to the zenith from
west to east. This may either be for want of
clouds or from excess of them on certain
sides.[110]

The "nature" that Thoreau's Journal describes or rather
translates in the medium of writing is movement, gravity, shape,
growth, decay, color, mass, atmosphere, and light–infinitely
substantiated by renewed perception.

Because the relation between the observer and the world
is largely freed from any commitment to connecting with
metaphysical truths, facts cease to be closed face-to-face
encounters between the spirit and the super-real, but unceasing
and open exchanges between an individual's consciousness and
the manifold plenitude of the material world. Thoreau's objects,
like Cézanne's Mont Sainte-Victoire, once disconnected from
any search for supra-reality, float immeasurably before us,
outside the world of defined locations, but nevertheless intensely
substantial. The Concord of Thoreau's Journal is no more
Concord than Cézanne's mountain is located near Aix-en-
Provence in southern France: it is both deeply material and
suffused with ontological reality.[111]

Experience as Instancing

Concomitant with a rejection of Platonist or Neo-
Platonic supra-reality comes a celebration of becoming as

---

[110] JXIII:109-11, including two rough sketches. Thoreau included
sketches or drawings in many of the late Journal's nature descriptions.
[111] Because Thoreau so deeply perceives nature as substance, he is no
post-modernist, even if he conceived nature as inseparable from the
constructive process of perception.

distinct from being.[112] Thoreau's purpose is emphatically not to talk of essences, but to devote himself to the presentness of things: "That which presents itself to us this moment occupies the whole of the present and rests on the very topmost point of the sphere, under the zenith."[113]

In the reciprocally constructed relationship between man and nature, Thoreau came to insist not only on the process of perception, but on nature itself as process: through "drenching" in time he aimed to keep himself awake to the immediacy of nature's temporally dissolving forms, like those he saw in the evening sky for example. Thoreau conceived of reality as process rather than as an entity circumscribed in a hierarchical and atemporal relation between the material and the spiritual. In the Journal of the 1850s, each entry is a celebration of the act of perception, and "facts" have become perceptual events–"My walk is so crowded with events–& phenomena."[114] Thoreau's unerring commitment to the natural world was meant to elicit particularity, not generalization, and he celebrates experience as instancing: "Ah give me pure mind–pure thought. Let me not be in haste to detect the *universal law,* let me see more clearly a particular instance..."[115]

Thoreau's endeavor was not to be "transported out of the district of change" or to make "Time and Space relations vanish"[116]–in other words to dissolve reality–but to engage with them, with the physicality of the world, to cleave to it even. Vision, for Thoreau, was synonymous, not with Emerson's moments when "the universe becomes transparent and the light of higher laws than its own shines *through* it,"[117] but with

---

[112] Neo-Platonic philosophy also envisioned a form of becoming, as phenomenal data were processed into a higher level of unity and spirituality, but it was an abstract, not a physical, becoming.

[113] JXIV:119-20; Oct. 13, 1860.

[114] J3:245; June 7, 1851.

[115] J4:223; Dec. 25, 1851.

[116] *Nature,* Emerson 2001, 47 and 40.

[117] Emerson 2001, 38, my emphasis.

encounters with the "thing itself," unmediated by any system or dogma. Extending the transcendentalist faith in the self-transcendence of the individual to the world itself, as the world answered the perceiver's awareness, Thoreau brought to its ultimate conclusion his recognition that "each object appears wholly undescribed to our experience."[118] What he sought was the timelessness of poetic or epiphanic experience, not the eternity of the symbol or the immutability of science's signs of reality. His search was for the moment when *chronos* becomes *kairos*[119]–*true* experience being at once timeless and timely:

> Some, seeing and admiring the neat figure of the
> hawk sailing two or three hundred feet above
> their heads, wish to get nearer and hold it in their
> hands, perchance, not realizing that they can see
> it best at this distance, *better now, perhaps, than
> ever they will again.*"[120]

Forsaking any search for truth behind or beyond appearances, Thoreau, through his Journal, sought not to control nature's reality, but to co-exist–perhaps even to be co-extensive–with it, to participate in its process. While he first envisioned a desirable facts-as-truth reduction, Thoreau progressively came to adopt a relatively detranscendentalized view[121]: he no longer

---

[118] J4:421; Apr. 2, 1852.

[119] I.e., time, instead of being conceived as a measurable (chronological) flow, is experienced as a significant moment, an occasion. (Ed.)

[120] JXIII:194-95; Mar. 15, 1860; my emphasis.

[121] Thoreau never ceased to define himself as a transcendentalist. It is interesting to note that, when he refused to join the Association for the Advancement of Science in 1853, he motivated his decision by an appeal to the apparently Emersonian faith "in a science which deals with the higher law," and described himself not as a scientist but as "a mystic–a transcendentalist & a natural philosopher to boot" (J5:469; Mar. 5, 1853). He then remarks that "a true account of my relation to nature should excite their ridicule only" (J5:470). That "true account"

sought representativity, but *instancing,* sensations and thoughts born of chance and situatedness:

> I see a small flock of blackbirds flying over, some rising, others falling, yet all advancing together, one flock but many birds, some silent, others tchucking,–incessant alternation. This harmonious movement as in a dance, this agreeing to differ, makes the charm of the spectacle to me. One bird looks fractional, naked, like a single thread or ravelling from the web to which it belongs. Alternation! Alternation! Heaven and hell! Here again in the flight of a bird, its ricochet motion, is that undulation observed in so many materials, as in the mackerel sky.[122]

Journal writing was above all for Thoreau the means to prolong and deepen his passage through life. *Passage,* it turns out, is the heart of Thoreau's work. Heeding the mobile, fluid, and luminous character of his experience, he spreads, divides, rhythmically marks, abundantly sweeps or stratifies time, producing a richly textured *timescape.* Thoreau's journal writing, like music, makes time perceptible. It dramatizes transitoriness, and to read his Journal is to engage with duration, succession and motion. What delights him in nature are the variations it plays on a theme: nature was indeed the central motif of his work, both in the musical sense of the word, and as his motivation or ground for living.

Thoreau was paradoxically empowered to reach maturity by an increasing sense of human finitude and of the limitations of all the tools meant to subjugate the physical world–whether

---

is the truth of his experience as recorded, not by any extrinsic work, but by the open-ended interweaving of world and consciousness offered by the Journal.

[122] JXII:44; Mar. 13, 1859.

esthetic, linguistic, or scientific. The Journal, as it questions any stable picture of the world and attempts to break with traditional notions of unity and harmony, rejects every kind of frame, and adopts instead a non-perspectival structure, which creates a new, many-faceted unity as a formal translation of nature. As for Thoreau's sense of the inadequacy of language, it is a logical consequence of his sense of the inadequacy of essences. Ultimately, the goal of comprehensiveness in science recedes before the recognition that no ultimate reality is possible, because of the fluid or dynamic character of knowledge. As a result Thoreau was bound to face the profoundly unsettling but rewarding indeterminacy of his engagement with the physical world: it is the very fact that nature ultimately resists our understanding that holds it open to continued perception and thus to freedom. In this respect Thoreau's Journal was not only a tool for perceiving, but for freedom–for achieving the poetic condition.

4

The Dwelling and the Labyrinth: Aspects of Being in the World in Thoreau's Journal

The past two decades of Thoreau studies have been characterized by an increased critical interest in the Journal, now becoming available in its entirety and specificity.[123] I do not propose here to retrace the major critics' views, much less to reposition the Journal in the architectural whole of Thoreau's work, but simply to make you want to plunge into the text itself, in all its density and complexity. To this end I have chosen to focus on a passage from an often neglected part of the Journal, composed after the publication of *Walden* and generally considered "dry."

This passage is neither representative nor exemplary. Its sole virtue is that it formalizes what I take to be the heart of the enterprise of the Journal. Studying it is therefore not a mere sounding of depths, but instead reveals the dynamics of this enormous whole, beyond the themes or problems to which it may give rise. I will also cite other passages which cast light upon this one, forming a living constellation over and above mere chronological order.

---

[123] I have in mind notably the thought-provoking works of Sharon Cameron and Daniel Peck, as well as, more generally, biographical studies by William Howarth and Robert D. Richardson: reevaluating Thoreau's evolution after *Walden*, they have stimulated a new interest in the Journal as a whole.

Since the ongoing Princeton Edition does not yet cover this period, I cite the text as given in the Torrey-Allen edition of 1906[124]:

As the afternoons grow shorter, and the early evening drives us home to complete our chores, we are reminded of the shortness of life, and become more pensive, at least in this twilight of the year. We are prompted to make haste and finish our work before the night comes. I leaned over a rail in the twilight on the Walden road, waiting for the evening mail to be distributed, when such thoughts visited me. I seemed to recognize the November evening as a familiar thing come round again, and yet I could hardly tell whether I had ever known it or only divined it. The November twilights just begun! It appeared like a part of a panorama at which I sat spectator, a part with which I was perfectly familiar just coming into view, and I foresaw how it would look and roll along, and prepared to be pleased. Just such a piece of art merely, though infinitely sweet and grand, did it appear to me, and just as little were any active duties required of me. We are independent on all that we see. The hangman whom I have *seen* cannot hang me. The earth which I have *seen* cannot bury me. Such doubleness and distance does sight prove. Only the rich and such as are troubled with ennui are implicated in the maze of phenomena. You cannot see anything until you are clear of it. The long railroad causeway through the meadows west of me, the still

---

[124] See footnote 2 in the preceding chapter.

twilight in which hardly a cricket was heard,[125] the dark bank of clouds in the horizon long after sunset, the villagers crowding to the post-office, and the hastening home to supper by candle-light, had I not seen all this before! What new sweet was I to extract from it? Truly they mean that we shall learn our lesson well. Nature gets thumbed like an old spelling-book. The almshouse and Frederick were still as last November. I was no nearer, methinks, nor further off from my friends. Yet I sat the bench with perfect contentment, unwilling to exchange the familiar vision that was to be unrolled for any treasure or heaven that could be imagined. Sure to keep just so far apart in our orbits still, in obedience to the laws of attraction and repulsion, affording each other only steady but indispensable starlight. It was as if I was promised the greatest novelty the world has ever seen or shall see, though the utmost possible novelty would be the difference between me and myself a year ago. This alone encouraged me, and was my fuel for the approaching winter. That we may behold the panorama with this slight improvement or change, this is what we sustain life for with so much effort from year to year.

And yet there is no more tempting novelty than this new November. No going to Europe or another world is to be named with it. Give me the old familiar walk, post-office and all, with this ever new self, with this infinite expectation and faith, which does not know when it is

---

[125] "Probably too cool for any these evenings; only in the afternoon." (Note by Thoreau.)

beaten. We'll go nutting once more. We'll pluck the nut of the world, and crack it in the winter evenings. Theatres and all other sightseeing are puppet-shows in comparison. I will take another walk to the Cliff, another row on the river, another skate on the meadow, be out in the first snow, and associate with the winter birds. Here I am at home. In the bare and bleached crust of the earth I recognize my friend.

One actual Frederick that you know is worth a million only read of. Pray, am I altogether a bachelor, or am I a widower, that I should go away and leave my bride? This Morrow that is ever knocking with irresistible force at our door, there is no such guest as that. I will stay at home and receive company.

I want nothing new, if I can have but a tithe of the old secured to me. I will spurn all wealth beside. Think of the consummate folly of attempting to go away from *here!* When the constant endeavor should be to get nearer and nearer *here.* Here are all the friends I ever had or shall have, and as friendly as ever. Why, I never had any quarrel with a friend but it was just as sweet as unanimity could be. I do not think we budge an inch forward or backward in relation to our friends. How many things can you go away from? They see the comet from the northwest coast just as plainly as we do, and the same stars through its tail. Take the shortest way round and stay at home. A man dwells in his native valley like a corolla in its calyx, like an acorn in its cup. *Here,* of course, is all that you love, all that you expect, all that you are. Here is your bride

elect, as close to you as she can be got. Here is
all the best and all the worst you can imagine.
What more do you want ? Bear hereaway then!
Foolish people imagine that what they imagine
is somewhere else. That stuff is not made in any
factory but their own.[126]

How can we untangle the skein formed by this passage
of extraordinary density? In it are mingled meditations on seeing
and dying, on the singularity of a place and the eternal return of
phenomena. Let's begin as Thoreau does, with seeing–"We are
independent on all that we see." This gaze, in other words, is
mine, but it doesn't depend on me. I am like a spectator watching
a reel unspooling before his eyes–a panorama. Or nowadays,
watching the projection of a film.[127] This is the permanent
cinema of nature. Our spectator, holding a ticket that seems
indefinitely valid, sees pictures which are perfectly familiar to
him, passing and re-passing. Or at least almost familiar. Is it
perfect familiarity if I hesitate between recognition ("whether I
had ever known it") and feeling ("or only divined it")? Perhaps
it's a familiarity which, after all, has no score to settle with the
mystery of the world. In any case, Thoreau affirms, I am not a
part of what I see. I am not its source, but its witness. In other
words the sovereignty of the fact, the independence of the
visible, is recognized. Because it is independent of us, after all,
we are independent of it.

Upon such a duality is vision based, this distance called
freedom. For make no mistake, only the demanding exercise of
freedom rescues this reciprocal independence from chaos. Only
the liberation of the gaze transforms the gardener into a poet: for

---

[126] JXI:273-75, Nov. 1, 1858. I have given above only a part of the
"whole" which comprises the full entries of November 1 and 2, 1858
(JXI:271-79), echoes of which will be found in the notes.
[127] The panorama, a very popular genre of the nineteenth century, was a
vast painted picture which was unrolled before the spectators in a
theatre, anticipating the age of the cinema. See Novak 20-24.

the gardener, the world is simple, it is divided into garden and "chaos, formless and lumpish."[128] Perhaps, Thoreau answers, yet that lump is a bed of flowers.

> When I rise to a hilltop, a thousand of these great oak roses, distributed on every side as far as the horizon! ... Now it is an extended forest or a mountain-side that bursts into bloom, through or along which we may journey from day to day. I admire these roses three or four miles off in the horizon. Comparatively, our gardening is on a petty scale, the gardener still nursing a few asters amid dead weeds, ignorant of the gigantic asters and roses which, as it were, overshadow him and ask for none of his care. ... Why not take more elevated and broader views, walk in the greater garden, not skulk in a little "debauched" nook of it? Consider the beauty of the earth, and not merely of a few impounded herbs? However, you will not see these splendors, whether you stand on the hilltop or in the hollow, unless you are prepared to see them. The gardener can see only the gardener's garden, wherever he goes. The beauty of the earth answers exactly to your demand and appreciation.[129]

---

[128] "We are not wont to see our dooryard as a part of the earth's surface. The gardener does not perceive that some ridge or mound in his garden or lawn is related to yonder hill or the still more distant mountain in the horizon, is, perchance, a humble spur of the last. We are wont to look on the earth still as a sort of chaos, formless and lumpish" (JXI:272; Nov. 1, 1858).

[129] JXI:277-78; Nov. 2, 1858.

The gardener is not independent of what he sees, for he connects it to the unity of an *idea*[130] of the world (the submission of nature to man). His world is subjective. He doesn't know or misunderstands the life that is characteristic of things: it is by his efforts that flowers grow and he doesn't see the trees flourish–"Comparatively," our gardening is on a petty scale, the gardener is still nursing a few asters amid dead weeds, ignorant of the gigantic asters and roses which, as it were, overshadow him and ask for none of his care." *His* world: he is indeed the owner of it, he has full power over it perhaps, whereas the poet–this unauthorized representative–takes his lessons from it – "Truly they mean that we shall learn our lesson well. Nature gets thumbed like an old spelling-book": a spelling book, to be sure, but also, if you will, a magical book of conjuring spells, though we know all its tricks by heart. Nature is that old school teacher who valiantly, from year to year, continues to teach you how to read words, to persevere in tracing, independently of your will, a form you haven't chosen–a sign that you belong to temporality. It's a long way from him who first Named–the image of his Creator but fallen from grace by his calamitous birthing of the feeble body of language[131]–to him who is determined to serve as the indefatigable witness of what is. And while the needy Adam, banished from Eden, is gardening the undergrowth, the poet, who doesn't recognize the day of his defeat–his resignation–persists in speaking. For in the final analysis, things cannot be distinguished from the event which produces them: to write the word, to say the name, is to recognize formally the life of things. Being reaches its climax in the writing of the Journal.

---

[130] "Surrounded by our thoughts or imaginary objects, living in our *ideas,* not one in a million ever sees the objects which are actually around him." (JXIII:137, Feb. 12, 1860. Thoreau's emphasis.)

[131] "It is impossible to describe the infinite variety of hues, tints, and shades, for the language affords no names for them, and we must apply the same term monotonously to twenty different things" (JXI:254-56, Oct. 27, 1858).

Here again we feel Thoreau's defiance in regard to all instituted activity–"You cannot see anything until you are clear of it." By the sectioning and the utilitarian standards that it imposes on the real, activity–having turned into use, function, labor–impoverishes it–a subjective vision of the world *par excellence*.[132] The gardener sees the mole that destroys his work and imperils his garden; the one the poet sees can neither destroy his work nor threaten his home. One man is independent from what he sees, the other not. To engage in an activity is to submit the world to the requirements of this activity. The poet doesn't constrain things to resemble him, he constrains them, by his *attention*, to exist–indefinitely carving out a form in the indeterminacy of this "formless and lumpish chaos." In the precariousness which is his luck and his destiny–"Only the rich and such as are troubled with ennui are implicated in the maze of phenomena"–the poet augments himself with that which is, "enriches himself" with the content of days.[133] Such is the reward of a detachment[134] which costs him everything the better to restore the infinite extent of his ties to the world.[135] The infinite which, as the whole Journal expounds, is found ever more closely in the folds of finitude, is opposed to the finite–at

---

[132] "We have only to elevate our view a little to see the whole forest as a garden" (JXI:267; Oct. 31, 1858).

[133] Compare this passage of Nov. 22, 1860: "It is glorious to consider how independent man is of all enervating luxuries; and the poorer he is in respect to them, the richer he is. Summer is gone with all its infinite wealth, and still nature is genial to man. Though he no longer bathes in the stream, or reclines on the bank, or plucks berries on the hills, still he beholds the same inaccessible beauty around him" (JXIV:259).

[134] Cf. the importance of the word "aloof" in this passage from *Walden*: "By a conscious effort of the mind we can stand aloof from actions and their consequences; and all things, good and bad, go by us like a torrent" (Thoreau 1971, 134).

[135] "Not till we are lost, in other words, not till we have lost the world, do we begin to find ourselves, and realize where we are and the infinite extent of our relations" (*Walden*, Thoreau 1971, 171).

once the boundary and the end of a process–as the poet is to the gardener.

To recognize the life of things. In a very beautiful passage, unfortunately too long to cite here,[136] the tree perceived acts, in fact, upon the perception; it creates, after a fashion, the space wherein it is pivotal–while the gardener, down at earth level, "sees only a few little asters." The world really perceived, Thoreau affirms clearly, has nothing to do with the definitions which seek to confine it. The world is a work which cannot be restricted. Its sovereignty is indivisible and necessary. Affirming this independence, it is of course essential to note, does not mean that that which is visible is pure exteriority. This independence defines the basis of poetic consciousness, its *sine qua non*. The text we are examining shows clearly the complexity of the connection which this consciousness has with the world, in that uncertain space between recognition and presentiment, and with being in its entirety. Here, with a lump in the throat, the spoken word more gravely informs us how serious existence is:

> This alone encouraged me, and was my fuel for the approaching winter. That we may behold the panorama with this slight improvement or change, this is what we sustain life for with so much effort from year to year.[137]

Here is evidence of how much effort the gaze, apparently passive, requires–a tension of one's entire being in order to harmonize with the movement of things, following the world's seemingly ineluctable rhythm. This is not a matter of submitting to a process that is ultimately external–indifferent, to us. Nor is it, as Daniel Peck maintains, an attempt to master its course. Rather, it is the attempt to incarnate its flow, to harmonize with its dynamics–this is the reason for those

---

[136] JXI:266-69, Oct. 31, 1858–the day before the passage specifically studied here.
[137] JXI:274, Nov. 1, 1858.

64

innumerable anticipations and backward glances which appear in
the Journal. For these dynamics, as we know, are not linear–are
not to be confused with the simple order of chronological
succession. They are a profusion which can be incarnated but not
put into words. More exactly, they find their only possible
expression in assent–in Thoreau's magnificent lines where hope
responds to promise, where his defiance of failure gathers
strength from the force of the eternal return. In the exultation of
consent, the chain is broken, the chain which binds us and
subjects us to the implacable revolution. How far away now
seems the doubt that gripped us at first: suppose what is offered
to–imposed upon?–our gaze is only stage scenery? This is not a
question of simply consenting to an identical reality–which
would be a form of resignation–but to a similar reality which is
ever surpassed by the promise of inexhaustibility.[138] Yet it is not
so much this infinite newness itself which motivates the consent;
rather it is the tacit renewal of the richness of the familiar, the
fortune of the everyday.

The other "thread" of our Journal passage is that this
consent also concerns space. Thoreau emphasizes his attachment
to place, to a "here" which is his only home–"A man dwells in
his native valley like a corolla in its calyx, like an acorn in its
cup." Distant places are always too beautiful to be true:

> Why does any distant prospect ever charm us?
> Because we instantly and inevitably imagine a
> life to be lived there such as is not lived
> elsewhere, or where we are. We presume that
> success is the rule. We forever carry a perfect
> sampler in our minds. Why are distant valleys,
> why lakes, why mountains in the horizon, ever
> fair to us? Because we realize for a moment that
> they may be the home of man, and that man's

---

[138] "Still he beholds the same inexhaustible beauty around him"
(JXIV:259).

life may be in harmony with them. Shall I say
that we thus forever delude ourselves?[139]

In the same breath we find then affirmed the indivisible
nature of our only inhabitable space-time: "And yet there's no
more tempting novelty than this new November. No going to
Europe or another world is to be named with it." Indeed we
cannot expect anything from a departure which would only be an
abandoning ("go away and leave"), an escape from time–in the
intoxication of a relatively fictitious world. That is why time and
place are so intimately linked in this passage: to leave is to lay
open the depth of an unreal and wholly other time, into which
that duration which is mine steals away. A blind gap, through
which we can glimpse and hope for a world behind appearances,
which thrives upon the demise of that which it supposedly
redeems. We become stripped of what we live for, of what
makes us live–the mystery, haunted by what is familiar yet never
quite the same ("with this slight improvement or change"), this
distance, this infinitely small space in which life is affirmed. The
dream–the *elsewhere*–always coincides with itself, since it has
no history.[140] No shadow surrounds it; it stands in the harsh light
of pure objectivity, dedicated to the anecdotal nature of tourism.
Tourism is indifference–Europe, "or another world." Everything
has the same value in the plurality of fictitious worlds. (They are
of course fictitious only for me who would go and visit them,
and not for those whose home they are[141]). Travel contains

---

[139] JXII:366-67, Oct. 3, 1859.

[140] In the same way, Thoreau, in his defense of John Brown, contrasts
true heroes with legendary figures: "A whole nation will for ages
cling to the memory of its Arthur, or other imaginary hero, who
perhaps never assailed its peculiar institution or sin, and being
imaginary, never failed ... while they forget their real heroes"
(JXII:405, Oct. 19, 1859).

[141] Cf.: "Why should we not stay at home? This is the land and we are
the inhabitants so many travellers come to see" (JXII:397, Oct. 17,
1859).

within it the idea that the voyage shall be profitable, as if it permitted us to gain something above that which each day brings ("All wealth beside"), by allowing us to escape from the repetition of the similar. As though it were a question of gaining ground along with gaining time. He who departs admits that the familiar no longer concerns him, that it has nothing more to do with him. The world isn't there for me, it is alien to me. Conversely, if I remain, it is because I am called to each of the things whose presence is ceaselessly renewed. They call to me exactly as much as I invoke them: "I will take another walk to the Cliff, another row on the river, another skate on the meadow, be out in the first snow, and associate with the winter birds." They visit me, seeming to exist only for me: "This Morrow that is ever knocking with irresistible force at our door, there is no such guest as that. I will stay at home and receive company."

The strength of this passage is that having begun with an apparent submission to what is happening, it finishes by thus revealing the power of assent–as if Thoreau were taking the initiative. As a result we may glimpse, little by little, an apparent beginning: as if, reaching a point beyond the ineluctable, it is Thoreau himself who is calling upon time to show itself, laying it open with a gesture in which the moment having reached its fullness, it overflows with infinite promise–a promise to remain *right here,* and permanently. This possible beginning exists because the world is rich with virtualities ("with this slight improvement or change"). Thanks to the virtual, things have a history and a beginning is possible. Virtuality, it should be emphasized, is not pure invention–it is nothing less than the life of things, the origin and endless renewal of what they are for me. These things are, then, not the distant objectivity implied in the image of the panorama; but they are *propositions of being*. I am the one who by taking hold of them–*taking* the initiative–gives them a historical dimension. The only history is human history; this is the essential principle by which "nature" is transformed into history. In other words–contrary to Peck's argument–the task of Thoreau's Journal is the conversion of space into time. If things did not have their virtuality, if they were external to all time, they would be reduced to being not what they are – i.e., a perpetual becoming –, but things which purely and simply are. This becoming, however, is rooted within them[142] and is the focus of my life; hence they have a history: "*Here*, of course, is all that you love, all that you expect, all that you are." I am these things whose being is an eternal proposition which I feel and approve–such is the double connection of being in the world, according to Thoreau. Being is thus grasped only in the form of its propositions, examined and observed. To the man who has once and for all determined their limits and meaning, things are only *things that are*; for the alert man, the poet, their being is inseparable from a historical becoming which is also his own. The world is what man's attention sets in motion: it has a history only because I am interested in it, because it proposes that I have something to do–to see, to hear, to feel.[143]

It is thus that death[144] is–temporarily–disarmed. Temporarily because we would have to be totally deaf not to hear, while reading along, the relatively sonorous echo produced by the difficulty of being, when being has to this extent been brought back into play. What we read here is only the most striking, the most readable, form of a sort of suspense in which

---

[142] "How they [grackles] sit and make a business of chattering! for it cannot be called singing, and no improvement from age to age perhaps. Yet, as nature is a becoming, their notes may become melodious at last" (JXIII:183, Mar. 8, 1860). Nature is a "becoming" in the Darwinian sense, which is Thoreau's meaning in the preceding citation. Yet certainly this becoming of things is the whole concern of the Journal, whether from day to day or through the ages.

[143] Cf. the essential passage of Oct. 13, 1860, quoted toward the beginning of Chapter 5 (JXIV:119-20).

[144] Death resounds too strongly in this text (notably in: "As the afternoons grow shorter, and the early evening drives us home to complete our chores, we are reminded of the shortness of life, and become more pensive, at least in this twilight of the year") for us not to hear an echo of All Saints' Day. (The passage is dated Nov. 1, 1858.)

all doubts and hopes cross each other's paths. Time suspended, stretched–an instant of vacancy which slips, which breaks the links of inevitability, breaks the grip of a reality which is overabundant and seemingly indifferent to man.

Here, almost in secret, the humble game of destiny is played. Everything happens as if the world was unfolding outside of me, but I had the good fortune of being able to catch my breath, one day or another–or a little each day–to establish a new beginning. In this return to intimacy–significantly, this is perhaps the simplest and most beautiful evocation of friendship in the Journal–we recover the strength to face reality again. Here is affirmed the ever-recurrent beginning of being. In this in-between, the heart accepts the promise of a perennial effort toward being, and renews the vows which proclaim anew its birth-cry.

As noted previously, the poet's precariousness is at once his strength and his destiny. We might hear an echo of religion in this–hardly surprising in a passage that also offers, as it were, the parable of two antithetical characters united chiefly in joylessness–"only the rich and such as are troubled with ennui are implicated in the maze of phenomena." The rich because they confuse the being of things with their price or their marketability,[145] or because, like the gardener, (who is rich, because he possesses *his* world, his vision of the world, even more than his garden), their activity lacks the necessary distance for seeing things. The jaded because, in contrast, their lack of activity, or more exactly their lack of propensity to act, is characterized by an infinite distance with relation to any object: the things are there, but, for lack of knowing where to get hold of them, for lack of being able to establish any relationship whatever with them, they are subject to their dominion, caught in their nets, enveloped in their folds ("implicated," Thoreau

---

[145] Compare, for example, these lines of Oct. 7, 1860: "Remarking to old Mr. B– the other day on the abundance of the apples, 'Yes,' says he, 'and fair as dollars too.' That's the kind of beauty they see in apples" (JXIV:103).

says).[146] The rich man and the bored man are both caught in the labyrinth of phenomena, not because they feel their profusion and get lost in them, but because their world, differently experienced, is immobile, fixed in its value or in its absence of value.[147]

That is why their relationship to the world lacks historical dimension or cannot really feel the force and the necessity of it. Indeed, how can I *feel* something that doesn't concern me? Either everything bores me, or else a thing is nothing more than the use made of it or the price paid for it. To the contrary, the very act of keeping a journal, as well as evolving the content of its pages, expresses a veritable passion– in every sense of the word, perhaps–for that which has a becoming, is inserted in time–"not realizing that they can see it best at this distance, better now, perhaps, than ever they will again"[148]

This should not lead us to discount the fascination exercised on Thoreau by the invariable, the apparent common denominator of the different occurrences of a "same" phenomenon.[149] It simply indicates that Thoreau in no way

---

[146] Deployment, on the other hand, is an essential aspect of Thoreau's Journal. The poet's vocation is to bring to light that which escapes perception because of the too great *compactness* of the world–this compactness or massiveness ("a sort of chaos, formless and lumpish") that the gardener seeks too easily to know by simply relegating it to the shadows of a *chaos* ("wilderness") determined by its name alone.

[147] "...the value of things generally is commonly estimated by the amount of money they will fetch. A thing is not valuable–e.g. a fine situation for a house–until it is convertible into so much money, that is, can cease to be what it is and become something else which you prefer" (JXIV:283, Nov. 29, 1860). See also a passage dated Oct. 13, 1860, on the value which people have universally, and from the beginning of time, attributed to gold (JXIV:118).

[148] JXIII:195, Mar. 15, 1860.

[149] Peck (1990, esp. 45-48) views the Journal as a document driven by a calendar-ideal, so to speak. This "culminate[d] in a set of charts, sometimes known as the 'Kalendar,' which he developed and drew up

primarily intends, by his explorations, to attain such an essence by reducing the facts themselves to ashes. There is indeed in the Journal a kind of immense and splendid combustion ("my fuel for the approaching winter"), but the stuff of life always won out over the magic brazier. To those ashen charts to which Peck seeks to reduce all that art and memory achieve, reply all these journal pages proclaiming the joy of seeing. Such is the reward offered him who, clinging to the taut cord of the present moment, of things untamed, refuses the comforting fixity of his relationship to the world, instead leaving his life open to those rude and tender shocks that jar the passing days.

---

near the end of his life, between 1860 and 1862." Peck discusses these seasonal or monthly charts as "an attempt to lay out all of nature's phenomena on a flat plane, that is, to graph their temporality and make a comprehensive picture of time" (47). This work, for Peck, is fundamental to Thoreau's strategic purpose in his search for truth–"a reflection of its [the Journal's] inherent purpose since at least 1852" (48).

5

Losing Sight of Oneself in What One Sees: Thoreau's Journal and Nature Writing

T horeau kept a singular sort of journal, as we have already seen. Far from keeping an intimate diary devoted to analyzing the twists and turns of individual personality, the author of *Walden* considered it his sole purpose, it seems, to explore the nature of the area surrounding Concord, Massachusetts. Maintained with admirable energy and steadfastness during 25 years of adult life–from October 22, 1837 to November 3, 1861, the Journal actually possess an uncommon dimension far exceeding its geographical and thematic limits. The interrogation of the same place patiently undertaken day after day, the resulting density, the methodical mining of reality, clearly prove that Thoreau's object is not the knowledge of nature as such, but an ontological and existential confrontation with the world. The line of force of Thoreau's Journal is not its documentary character; rather, each of its elements is the irrepressible uprising of an inherent force. Whether the content describes plants, birds, and landscapes or involves political reflections, this force is the locus of everything which, rejecting the preconceived determinants and conventional ties of man with the world–struggling, battling against the inevitable backfire of old habits of thought, intent on revealing the unspoken–bears the entire destiny of the free individual. Thoreau's approach then is highly metaphysical, not by what it states–for it never goes beyond realities–but by the very nature of its commitment. The metaphysical character of the Journal is not an intention but a fact. The reader in a hurry will perhaps see in the Journal only an interminable litany of plant names or descriptions. That is to confuse, among other simplifications, the gesture and the meaning of the gesture. The word or the sentence, in the Journal do not designate–do not constitute the real in signs. If they show something, it is not only what one thinks one recognizes. Words here are above all a formidable hand-to-hand struggle with things, with the time it takes to appropriate them–a time supremely nestled in Thoreau's sometimes "dry" text–with their mysterious familiarity. It is not Concord that Thoreau describes–the Journal could almost be captioned, "this is not Concord." Thoreau, like Cézanne painting Mont Sainte-Victoire over and over throughout his life, explores the complexity of the links and the processes by which, in and through man, the visible is elaborated. In other words, the place only *takes the place* of an unlocatable confrontation with the world.

The Spacing of the World

Of course overturning systems and hierarchies, as required in this confrontation, demands a considerable effort, the abandonment of all proprieties. Yet it is nothing compared to the moment when these masks are torn from reality, and the emperor stands revealed without clothing:

> In the true natural order the order or system is not insisted on. Each is first, and each last. That which presents itself to us this moment occupies the whole of the present and rests on the very topmost sphere, under the zenith. The species and individuals of all the natural kingdoms ask our attention and admiration in a round robin. We make straight lines, putting a captain at their head and a lieutenant at their tails, with sergeants and corporals all along the line and a flourish of trumpets near the beginning, insisting on a particular uniformity where Nature has

> made curves to which belongs their own sphere-
> music. It is indispensable for us to square her
> circles, and we offer our rewards to him who
> will do it.[150]

Ah, this joyous ring of petitioners! Each one stands up and demands the complete attention of a poet quite disconcerted at having thus opened the sack of winds. Now here he is, entirely exposed to this reality crowding around and calling his name from the four corners of the horizon. Or rather from all around the circumference of the world. This liberation of beings signals the coming of uniqueness, the preeminence of individuals over the system. Yet the farewell to systems and definitions, to every kind of organized procedure, does not end up in an anarchy which would be the swift ruin of all this life. The poet's faith, his madness even, is that the things vying for his admiration form a circle around him. The circle is the image of a strict equality of position, that is, of status, among things. It is the opposite of a field of orderly lines that keeps everything in its place by military rank. Against the hierarchy, and against anarchy, democracy. So we have not just removed one set of conventions in order to establish another one.

Let us look again at the poet's objects. They do not line up behind him, but make a circle around him. Or rather, they make a circle. To be exact, the poet is not the compass point tracing the world (that is the privilege of God, whose center is everywhere and circumference nowhere), but stands outside the circle of things–the logical consequence of his prime task, relinquishing the world. Man and the world are then nothing more than two spheres meeting on one almost dimensionless point–this "most extreme point of the sphere," a magnificent image affirming this tension of the real toward man, who responds with a forward movement of his whole being, all his involvement. One is reminded of "The Creation of Adam" in the

---

[150] JXIV:119-20, Oct. 13, 1860.

Sistine Chapel. When God created man, having completed the world, wasn't it simply to claim "attention and admiration" from this being who was already there–God has no history–and was just dozing? To see, in a sense, is to be created anew. And created in the image of what we see.

But what do we actually see? This world, in which each of us is at once first and last, is in reality too dense to be seen. Where to begin, where finish, now that there is no order any more? It would be too good if the moment alone could define the form of the gaze. The present, Thoreau tells us, is that which presents itself to us at a given moment–as long as we understand that what presents itself must be grasped lest it remain a dead letter–seized and made to say what it is, to reveal what is hidden in it. The poet's vocation then is to bring to light what escapes our perception owing to the too great compactness of the world. Not to unveil essences, but to unfold or space out these appearances that cover each other, all of them claiming exclusive attention, all of them promising a joy that is imperiled by their own undertow. To see is, then, this subtle drifting in the mixed waters of the instant and of history, of place and of space: "The tree which looked comparatively lifeless, cold, and merely parti-colored, seen in a more favorable light as you are floating away from it, may affect you wonderfully as a warm, glowing drapery."[151] Not designing new hierarchies, but getting into the heart of the tension between what is before you and what resists being perceived. It does not matter to the "gardener," the man engaged in practical action, that the world is too massive ("formless and lumpish"[152]). It is not possible for him to stay there so long as things all appear in good order–a seamless order that screens what he does not want to see, what is too simple to see as he sees it. He uses measured words, laid out according to their usefulness, which cast these objects far from their share of the light. He is one of those who make "straight lines"–hedges and enclosures frame the furrows he is digging. The army of

[151] JXIV:107-08.
[152] JXI:272.

words, like the army of things, has to toe his line. As for the words of the scientist, they are just as measured, his language just as "guarded":

> After all, the truest description, and that by which another living man can most readily recognize a flower, is the unmeasured and eloquent one which the sight of it inspires. ... Which are the truest, the sublime conceptions of Hebrew poets and seers, or the guarded statements of modern geologists, which we must modify or unlearn so fast?[153]

True description is "the unmeasured and eloquent one which the sight of [the object] inspires." It is probably no mere coincidence if this idea of an "unmeasured" yet spoken description coincides with the disappearance, after 1850, of versified poetry in Thoreau's work. The poetic condition can also mean abandoning a "poetic" form that is too rhythmical and–precisely–too measured. Thoreau wasn't trying to compete with music. The only rhythm which counts is the deployment of a reality in which the object suddenly occupies the extreme point of the sphere–like a unique protuberance breaking the indeterminacy of time and sight. And, if "appearances are deceptive,"[154] it is never because they mask the being of things–a mythical and "objective" being-in-itself, but because they enfold their temporality or their historicity.

The world, fundamentally, is indeed like a text, but it is too dense, too compact: the writer's task is to put some space

---

[153] JXIV:117; Oct. 13, 1860.

[154] "Truly, appearances are deceptive," Thoreau declares of a "pine wood" that actually contains many more oaks than pines on closer examination. Making himself the witness of a becoming, seeing the world as if he were reading a history book, he sees through well-ordered appearances. Such are the "practical" implications of a metaphysical rule.

into it, some room to move about, to get free of the labyrinth of reality and its folds and creases–the "maze of phenomena" in which "only the rich and such as are troubled with ennui are implicated."[155]

Unspoken, the world is "formless, lumpish" chaos, uninhabitable.[156] The gardener lives only on its edges, even if his words seek to persuade us that he occupies the center. To speak is what heals a bruised language, suspected of missing things. To speak is to aerate the texture of the world: "Let us make distinctions."[157] Not, as a certain idealistic poetry would have it, to gather its scattered fragments together, but quite the contrary, to explode its too great compactness–which also is its mutism. The world doesn't speak to whoever wants to hear it, not even to the one who knows how to hear it, but to the one who is determined to snatch from it a few words sealed in a compact order. To be a poet, to work at the summit of indiscipline, is not to unmask the visible (that is just the most immediate operation, the simplest: having rid discourse of sclerosis, and activity of order, and to find oneself in a position of openness, of availability), but rather to face the visible, at the greatest intensity of vision, in order to make it inhabitable. The day is formless–a block whose gaze diminishes its indeterminacy. The day, the world, are a plenitude which has nothing to do with me. Not because there is a meaning that is dormant, hidden in it,

---

[155] JXI:273.

[156] "We are wont to look on earth still as a sort of chaos, formless and lumpish" (JXI:272). The gardener does not say the world, but designates it, his imparting of form amounts to erecting two contradictory wholes, the exterior of his territory appearing as the other, the formless. The poet, refusing these partitions (the whole, integrity, occupy a central place in Thoreau's thought), by his attention and admiration, gives form and life to that which is. The poet is a traitor who, relieving the gardener of guard duty, ventures into the forbidden space. While the gardener has given up on this too compact world, from which he seeks to protect himself by confining it to the "formless," the poet remains unreconciled.

[157] JXIV:228.

which the right incantations will awaken and bring to light. It is rather because, by being too visible–as though overexposed–it may no longer be seen. To see, to feel, is to try to put distance between things, not a fixed, angular, distance, as in common perception, but room to sense the breathing of things, to behold the heartbeat of being.

The poetic word makes room for silence–which does not mean absence of expression: the writer who, from his retreat, interprets a score already written, gives life to a voice other than his own. Via the discontinuity of his Journal, Thoreau, like a musician, becomes the interpreter of a characteristically human structure–for it incorporates silence, pauses, imaginary voids which temporarily relax the grip of the world. Assuming the role of poet, Thoreau has chosen to confront a world saturated with being, so very full that he has to loosen its strong embrace. To read the world is to unscramble its illegible signs, to investigate the signs of an uncertain language, ever dreaming of a direct and total reading of "the book of Nature"–not to arrange the signs neatly, but, seizing them, to feel the roughness of their too emotionless geology.

Going Through Language

If the world at first is also, for the poet, formless, it is because the given, the *a priori*, has been, not sanctioned, but placed outside our scope–the poet is always just the gardener laid bare. To read, recognize a form, unfold the signs of the visible which must constantly be redefined and of a history which must be constructed (thus affording us something to do), of a future to imagine[158]–is a way of reconciling oneself with a world in disgrace, and constantly menaced with destruction: violence arises where the word is missing. And if I don't know how to seize things, how to make them mine, then a violent act, cutting

---

[158] This is the counterpart, in the realm of action, of the thrust of Thoreau's esthetics.

to the quick, will subjugate them. To assure the percolation of language into the compactness of the world, and to take hold of realities–gently yet with determination and commitment–are two perfectly equivalent operations. It is disengagement which fosters violence. Once the hierarchies and the conventions are abolished, man and things stand as equal to equal. Hence engagement, hence this amorous dance with things, which remains impossible so long as hedges and screens crop up, so long as we are not freed from the labyrinth of the real. Dancing between two infinities, free at the risk of his fallible vision, moving toward things rather than constraining them to come to him, the poet belongs to a world which he feels as an infinity of propositions of being, which are his to seize:

> Unconsidered expressions of our delight which any natural object draws from us are something complete and final in themselves, since all nature is to be regarded as it concerns man.[159]

"All nature is to be regarded as it concerns man." Clearly, for Thoreau, it is never a question of dehumanizing the world and sending man back to his brutish sleep. To insert space in the world is thus to prevent nature, which never fails to take back the slightest bit of lost ground, from attracting man into her wild bosom–opening him up to a violence of which she would be the first victim. No one is closer, in fact, to the state of nature than this crude and poorly formed, indeed lumpish, creature, the gardener, whose surface culture (in every sense of the term)

---

[159] JXIV:117; Oct. 13, 1860. When Thoreau, as a moralist, attacks the greed of his contemporaries, and of men in general, he is attacking greed for all things that pay back, that fetch a return. Joy does not fetch anything except itself, and the one who experiences it is rich in absolute value. It is not by chance that we find in Thoreau's Journal on the same day a reflection on the absolute value (immeasurable) of joy, and considerations on the fluctuations (measurable) of the value of gold.

seems his genius. About man's so-called culture, Thoreau waxes ironic:

> What sort of cultivation, or civilization and improvement, is ours to boast of, if it turns out that, as in this instance, unhandselled nature is worth more even by our modes of valuation than our improvements are,–if we leave the land poorer than we found it?[160]

For the poet, facing the world is indissolubly linked to the question of language and knowledge. One of Thoreau's deepest intuitions is to have realized that man could hope to be really present in the world only by holding himself at the balance point between knowledge and ignorance. Throughout the 1850s, the years of his burning desire to see without constraint, Thoreau recorded in his Journal a number of reflections on the necessity of learning the name and at the same time forgetting it, of knowing and not knowing:

> I have known a particular rush, for instance, for at least twenty years, but have ever been prevented from describing some [of] its peculiarities, because I did not know its name nor any one in the neighborhood who could tell me it. With the knowledge of the name comes a more distinct recognition and knowledge of the thing. That shore is now more describable, and poetic even. My knowledge was cramped and confined before, and grew rusty because not used,–for it could not be used. My knowledge now becomes communicable and grows by communication. I can now learn what others know about the same thing.[161]

---

[160] JXIV:229; Nov. 10, 1860.
[161] JXI:137, Aug. 29, 1858.

> How much of beauty–of color, as well as form–on which our eyes daily rest goes unperceived by us! No one but a botanist is likely to distinguish nicely the different shades of green with which the open surface of the earth is clothed,–not even a landscape-painter if he does not know the species of sedges and grasses which paint it. With respect to the color of grass, most of those even who attend peculiarly to the aspects of Nature only observe that it is more or less dark or light, green or brown, or velvety, fresh or parched, etc. But if you are studying grasses you look for another and different beauty, and you find it, in the wonderful variety of color, etc., presented by the various species.[162]

For Thoreau, knowing the name of a thing–knowing the name *and* the thing–was at once necessary and dangerous. We can see only what we have first learned to recognize, but then we run a great risk of substituting what we know for what we perceive. So learning must be only a step, a beginning that is certainly necessary but that also has limits which must be respected. Again and again, Thoreau affirms that we will see only when we have forgotten what we know, when the masks of ignorance have fallen away, when we lose sight of all that imposes itself in place of things, all that leads the gaze astray, sends it in the wrong direction. "We have such a habit of looking away that we see not what is around us."[163] I am dispossessed of things by their name; so I must give up the name in order to recover the world:

---

[162] JXIV:3, Aug. 1, 1860.
[163] JXIII:141.

It is only when we forget all our learning that we begin to know. I do not get nearer by a hair's breadth to any natural object so long as I presume that I have an introduction to it from some learned man. To conceive of it with a total apprehension I must for the thousandth time approach it as something totally strange. If you would make acquaintance with the ferns you must forget your botany. You must get rid of what is commonly called knowledge of them. Not a single scientific term or distinction is the least to the purpose, for you would fain perceive something, and you must approach the object totally unprejudiced. You must be aware that no thing is what you have taken it to be. In what book is this world and its beauty described? Who has plotted the steps toward the discovery of beauty? You have got to be in a different state from common. Your greatest success will be simply to perceive that such things are...[164]

We are as often injured as benefited by our systems, for, to speak the truth, no human system is a true one, and a name is at most a mere convenience and carries no information with it. As soon as I begin to be aware of the life of any creature, I at once forget its name. To know the names of creatures is only a convenience to us at first, but so soon as we have learned to distinguish them, the sooner we forget their names, the better, so far as any true appreciation of them is concerned.[165]

---

[164] JXII:371; Oct. 4, 1859.
[165] JXIII:155, Feb. 18, 1860.

> Whatever aid is to be derived from the use of a scientific term, we can never begin to see anything as it is so long as we remember the scientific term which always our ignorance has imposed on it. Natural objects and phenomena are in this sense forever wild and unnamed by us.[166]

Thoreau describes a fertile forgetting which consecrates the inexhaustible ebb and flow of presence. Presence–things just as they are ("anything as it is")–necessarily escapes the grip of language; we are kept in a wilderness forever unexplored. As Thoreau famously declared, "The frontiers are not east or west, north or south, but wherever a man *fronts* a fact, though that fact be his neighbor, there is an unsettled wilderness between him and Canada, between him and the setting sun, or, farther still, between him and *it*."[167] Wilderness is the inexhaustible. So the border is thus not in space but in time: "Natural objects and phenomena are in this sense forever wild and unnamed by us."[168] The world of presence is unnamed: language is not the instrument of saying; it only allows us to dissipate vagueness by instituting differences. Before Thoreau dismisses terminology, his eye must have assimilated these differences, or rather, it must have assimilated their principle, in order to see them without the paltry help of words. This proposal, in its modesty, denies all romantic pretension: not believing in language as it exists any more than in its glorious reform, infinitely distrusting it, it deprives it of its mission to say the world. At most its mission is to greet presence with a gesture devoid of all bitterness, to bow wisely before the forever unnamed, unnamable, heart of things–their "effluence."[169] Saying the name is recognizing the life of

---

[166] JXIII:141, Feb. 12, 1860.

[167] Thoreau 1980b, 304.

[168] JXIII:141.

[169] Cf.: "The ultimate expression or fruit of any created thing is a fine effluence which only the most ingenious worshipper perceives at a

things – and acknowledging thus its belonging to the world. For these things, once the shaking rattles of words are abandoned, are literally, what touches me – what involves me. And no more than words can say what I am, can shatter the signal of my name, no more can this relationship which links me to things be said. Saying the name is acknowledging the life of things: it is an act of acknowledgment which signals my presence to and in them, their presence to and for me. He who designates something disengages himself from it. The poet does not designate, but signs the document of a common presence, the deed of what Paul Claudel, in a play on words, called *co-naissance* (a knowing which is a co-birth), emphasizing thus the reciprocal engendering of the person and things, and drawing attention to a creation which is always a starting point, the possibility of a beginning ("forever wild and unnamed"), movement of and toward this unknown which will always precede us (as I discussed in Chapter 4). The poet is eager, but may never be able, to register, to transcribe being. He walks a tightrope, testing his movement while completely exposed, lacking the support of a secure and confident tread, defying with each step the chasm that awaits. The poet's act of seeing presumes his constantly vertiginous acceptance of the void. This acceptance is purchased at a great price, at the end of a struggle taken up again and again, where the affirmation of the vow of poverty barely carries the day against the dream of a richer language. The richness of language is actually an obstacle, presenting the temptation to play with it, to take pleasure in cultivating it for its own sake, when the real challenge is to be ever nearer to the world. It seems that in the latter years of Thoreau's Journal a profound struggle has gone on between the security of words and the promise of the world, a prolonged confrontation in which language becomes situated and the poet affirmed by his spoken

---

reverent distance from its surface even. The cause and the effect are equally evanescent and intangible, and the former must be investigated in the same spirit and with the same reverence with which the latter is perceived" (XII:23, Mar. 7, 1859).

word, even as he claims that, anyhow, he doesn't believe all that much in words.

Language advances openly, ahead of rejected definitions. Can we believe that this would be the case on every page? Lovers of spectacle would have it so. But this puritan wants nothing to do with spectacle. Being, not entertaining, is his task, whether he explicitly took it on or not. He is entirely devoted to interrogation, to plunging into the supreme fiction[170] of total abandon, guided only by his own marks–as if the surveyor had decided all of a sudden to survey without triangulating from established points, and drew a pure space confounded with his drawing of it. The territory would coincide, then, exactly with the map, with the gesture of the surveyor; it would be the sum of his gestures. Hence Thoreau's vision of a pyramid resting on its point–speech, having dismissed words, arises from a point without dimension, clinging to the mobile and variable support offered by experience:

> We touch our subject but by a point which has
> no breadth, but the pyramid of our experience,
> or our interest in it, rests on us by a broader or
> narrower base. That is, man is all in all, Nature
> nothing, but as she draws him out and reflects
> him.[171]

Poetic speech, like an inverted pyramid, operates in the forgetting of the word and advances toward the bright flash of presence, of a common presence. Some morose minds, realists, will claim that a pyramid cannot stand on its point, failing to see how it is collectively stabilized by the community of readers–or by the solitary madman dancing with the wind so as to hang on to the stays.

---

[170] Wallace Stevens's expression for the poet's accomplishment. Cf. "Notes Toward a Supreme Fiction" (Stevens 380-408).

[171] JIX:121, Oct. 18, 1856.

"Man is all in all, Nature nothing"

To the idea that the Journal "says" nature for itself, all meaning for man set aside,[172] must be opposed the existential intensity evident on every page of the Journal (however arid certain readers may sometimes find them)–Thoreau's emphasis on his joy in the spectacle of the world, and the many passages wherein he underlines the fact that things have meaning only in relation to man, "since all nature is to be regarded as it concerns man."[173] Cameron describes the Journal in formalist terms, analyzing only the forms of the visible and of writing, while losing sight of Thoreau's connection of esthetic to ethical concerns. It is indeed in relation to man that the world must be thought, but this relationship must itself be thought on other grounds than the usual: we must not confuse working to lose sight of oneself in what one sees, and working to "represent" a nature unrelated to man. Thoreau works to achieve a mode of seeing that cannot be misled by criteria of convenience or psychologism. His work has nothing to do with either the rules of action or the projection of feelings, but with the ontological situation of man. In other words, Cameron has confused Thoreau's rejection of the idea of the conventional, one-dimensional relationship of man to the world, with the abandonment of any relationship or the subordination of man to nature considered in itself–which can certainly turn out to be a useful, necessary or productive exercise, but could in no case bring closure, or serve as a goal. Thoreau is not a sage who

---

[172] Sharon Cameron has opened new avenues of thought on the Journal with her complex analysis in *Writing Nature* (1985). Yet she emphasizes the Journal's techniques for marginalizing human content, Thoreau supposedly being intent on recording "phenomena [that] are dissociated from human significance" (75) and are bound in a self-referentiality. Thoreau, Cameron states, sought "to see nature contrastively not against the background of human concerns, but rather against aspects of itself" (66).

[173] JXIV:117.

would withdraw from the world, but a man determined to reside fully in it, having procured the spiritual means to do so.[174]

Thus the Journal's purpose is not so much "writing nature" in and for itself than to conceive and embody the poetic condition in all its complexity, omitting neither uncertainties nor ambiguities. For the same reason, one cannot subscribe to Peck's analysis of the Journal's final years: "In 1851, Thoreau was approaching the final decade of his life, and this decade was given to the most intense search for nature's meanings ever undertaken by an American writer. The Journal is a record of that search."[175] To the contrary, it would appear that Thoreau at that point renounced any search for meaning in nature (if it ever was his primary purpose), recognizing rather that it is our task to live in the world, simply but truly, and that the essential question is that of the meaning of our life. Exercising his vision unceasingly in pursuit of singularity (old habits are hard to shake), the poet sculpts the formlessness of the day, unceasingly inaugurates time,[176] pursuing a labor which delves into grief as much as joy, but by accepting it, makes sense of death. "Be it life or death, we crave only reality".[177]

---

[174] I concur here with Michel Granger, who emphasizes that Thoreau's "relationship to nature, paradoxically, becomes the privileged point from which to reflect upon the meaning of the human condition" (233). Contrary to Cameron's non-humanist reading of Thoreau, I believe it is essential to insist upon the profound humanism of his thinking.

[175] Peck 1993, xix.

[176] Peck 1990, 156-157.

[177] *Walden,* Thoreau 1971, 98.

6

Emerson's Literary Ethics

Against the current of an era which saw the rise of the novel as a major literary form in both the United States and Europe, the Transcendentalists in the period 1830-1850 had an aversion to fiction and resolutely ignored it. These heirs of the Puritans and more directly of Unitarianism showed a preference for different, more traditional genres of prose, notably the essay, autobiography and travel narrative, which alone could satisfy their aspiration toward a literature whose prime vocation would be to reveal and to inspire. In the work of their central figure, Ralph Waldo Emerson, esthetics, far from being autonomous, remained largely subordinate to a moral aim, an ethical project on which it was based and which gave it legitimacy. This is the subject I wish to sketch here–Emerson's pragmatics as a writer–focusing on his *Essays*.

Rhetoric of Provocation

I must first demonstrate what the force and efficacy of Emerson's writing owes to rhetoric, the essential role played in the production of meaning, by linking the elements of a discourse whose modes of operation and complex interplay comprise what may be called "staging."

Fundamentally, three systems of discourse characterize the essays and speeches of Emerson–disjunction, injunction, and conjunction. I broadly call disjunction the writer's mode of creating a break in the order of the discourse or the statement; injunction, the mode of the imperative tense and the exhortation; and conjunction, the mode in which the tensions created by the play of the first two are abolished or transcended. The beginning of the essay "History" provides examples of these three modes of discourse. This is the first of Emerson's *Essays: First Series*, published in 1841.

Although not the best known or the most polished of Emerson's essays, it interests me for the particular readability of its rhetorical structure. I wish to look especially closely at the opening paragraphs, reproduced here:

> There is one mind common to all individual men. Every man is an inlet to the same and to all of the same. He that is once admitted to the right of reason is made a freeman of the whole estate. What Plato has thought, he may think; what a saint has felt, he may feel; what at any time has befallen any man, he can understand. Who hath access to this universal mind is a party to all that is or can be done, for this is the only and sovereign agent.

> Of the works of this mind history is the record. Its genius is illustrated by the entire series of days. Man is explicable by nothing less than all his history. Without hurry, without rest, the human spirit goes forth from the beginning to embody every faculty, every thought, every emotion, which belongs to it in appropriate events. But the thought is always prior to the fact; all the facts of history preëxist in the mind as laws. Each law in turn is made by circumstances predominant, and the limits of nature give power to but one at a time. A man is the whole encyclopædia of facts. The creation of a thousand forests is in one acorn, and Egypt, Greece, Rome,

Gaul, Britain, America, lie folded already in the first man. Epoch after epoch, camp, kingdom, empire, republic, democracy, are merely the application of his manifold spirit to the manifold world.

This human mind wrote history, and this must read it. The Sphinx must solve her own riddle. If the whole of history is in one man, it is all to be explained from individual experience. There is a relation between the hours of our life and the centuries of time. As the air I breathe is drawn from the great repositories of nature, as the light on my book is yielded by a star a hundred millions of miles distant, as the poise of my body depends on the equilibrium of centrifugal and centripetal forces, so the hours should be instructed by the ages, and the ages explained by the hours. Of the universal mind each individual man is one more incarnation. All its properties consist in him. Each new fact in his private experience flashes a light on what great bodies of men have done, and the crises of his life refer to national crises. Every revolution was first a thought in one man's mind, and when the same thought occurs to another man, it is the key to that era. Every reform was once a private opinion, and when it shall be a private opinion again, it will solve the problem of the age. The fact narrated must correspond to something in me to be credible or intelligible. We as we read must become Greeks, Romans, Turks, priest and king, martyr and executioner, must fasten these images to some reality in our secret experience, or we shall learn nothing rightly. What befell Asdrubal or Cæsar Borgia is as much an illustration of the mind's powers and depravations as what has befallen us. Each new law and political movement has meaning for you. Stand before each of its tablets and say, 'Under this mask did my Proteus nature hide itself.' This remedies the defect of our too great nearness to ourselves. This throws our actions into perspective: and as crabs, goats, scorpions, the balance, and the waterpot lose their meanness when hung as signs in the zodiac, so I can see my own vices without heat in the distant persons of Solomon, Alcibiades, and Catiline.

It is the universal nature which gives worth to particular men and things. Human life as containing this is mysterious and inviolable, and we hedge it round with penalties and laws. All laws derive hence their ultimate reason; all express more or less distinctly some command of this supreme, illimitable essence. Property also holds of the soul, covers great spiritual facts, and instinctively we at first hold to it with swords and laws, and wide and complex combinations. The obscure consciousness of this fact is the light of all our day, the claim of claims; the plea for education, for justice, for charity, the foundation of friendship and love, and of the heroism and grandeur which belong to acts of self-reliance. It is remarkable that involuntarily we always read as superior beings. Universal history, the poets, the romancers, do not in their stateliest pictures–in the sacerdotal, the imperial palaces, in the triumphs of will or of genius–anywhere lose our ear, anywhere make us feel that we intrude, that this is for better men; but rather is it true, that in their grandest strokes we feel most at home. All that Shakespeare says of the king, yonder slip of a boy that reads in the corner feels to be true of himself. We sympathize in the great moments of history, in the great discoveries, the great resistances, the great prosperities of men;– because there law was enacted, the sea was searched, the land was found, or the blow was struck *for us*, as we ourselves in that place would have done or applauded.

We have the same interest in condition and character. We honor the rich, because they have externally the freedom, power, and grace which we feel to be proper to man, proper to us. So all that is said of the wise man by Stoic, or oriental or modern essayist, describes to each reader his own idea, describes his unattained but attainable self. All literature writes the character of the wise man. Books, monuments, pictures, conversation, are portraits in which he finds the lineaments he is forming. The silent and the eloquent praise him and accost him, and he is stimulated wherever he moves as by personal allusions. A true aspirant, therefore, never needs look for allusions personal and laudatory in discourse. He hears the commendation, not of himself, but more sweet, of that character he seeks, in every word that is said concerning character, yea, further, in every fact and circumstance,–in the running river and the rustling corn. Praise is looked, homage tendered, love flows from mute nature, from the mountains and the lights of the firmament.

These hints, dropped as it were from sleep and night, let us use in broad day. The student is to read history actively and not passively; to esteem his own life the text, and books the commentary. Thus compelled, the Muse of history will utter oracles, as never to those who do not respect themselves. I have no expectation that any man will read history aright, who thinks that what was done in a remote age, by men whose names have resounded far, has any deeper sense than what he is doing to-day.

The world exists for the education of each man. There is no age or state of society or mode of action in history, to which there is not somewhat corresponding in his life. Every thing tends in a wonderful manner to abbreviate itself and yield its own virtue to him. He should see that he can live all history in his own person. He must sit solidly at home, and not suffer himself to be bullied by kings or empires, but know that he is greater than all the geography and all the government of the world; he must transfer the point of view from which history is commonly read, from Rome and Athens and London to himself, and not deny his conviction that he is the court, and if England or Egypt have any thing to say to him, he will try the case; if not, let them for ever be silent. He must attain and maintain that lofty sight where facts yield their secret sense, and poetry and annals are alike. The instinct of the mind, the purpose of nature, betrays itself in the use we make of the signal narrations of history. Time dissipates to shining ether the solid angularity of facts. No anchor, no cable, no fences, avail to keep a fact a fact. Babylon, Troy, Tyre, Palestine, and even early Rome, are passing already into fiction. The Garden of Eden, the sun standing still in Gibeon, is poetry thenceforward to all nations. Who cares what the fact was, when we have made a constellation of it to hang in heaven an immortal sign? London and Paris and New York must go the same way. "What is History," said Napoleon, "but a fable agreed upon?" This life of ours is stuck round with Egypt, Greece, Gaul, England, War, Colonization, Church, Court, and Commerce, as with so many flowers and wild ornaments grave and gay. I will not make more account of them. I believe in Eternity. I can find Greece, Asia, Italy, Spain, and the Islands,–the genius and creative principle of each and of all eras in my own mind.

We are always coming up with the emphatic facts of history in our private experience, and verifying them here. All history becomes subjective; in other words, there is properly no history; only biography. Every mind must know the whole lesson for itself,–must go over the whole ground. What it does not see, what it does not live, it will not know. What the former age has epitomized into a formula or rule for manipular convenience, it will lose all the good of verifying for itself, by means of the wall of that rule. Somewhere, sometime, it will demand and find compensation for that loss by doing the work itself. Ferguson discovered many things in astronomy which had long been known. The better for him.

History must be this or it is nothing. Every law which the state enacts indicates a fact in human nature; that is all. We must in ourselves see the necessary reason of every fact,–see how it could and must be. So stand before every public and private work; before an oration of Burke, before a victory of Napoleon, before a martyrdom of Sir Thomas More, of Sidney, of Marmaduke Robinson, before a French Reign of Terror, and a Salem hanging of witches, before a fanatic Revival, and the Animal Magnetism in Paris, or

94

in Providence. We assume that we under like influence should be alike affected, and should achieve the like; and we aim to master intellectually the steps, and reach the same height or the same degradation, that our fellow, our proxy, has done.[178]

"History" begins with the affirmation of a central theme of Emerson's thought: "There is one mind common to all individual men." This declaration seems to hover supernaturally over the discourse that it introduces. By force of affirmation, the speaker establishes his legitimacy–his right to take the floor. The paradox, however, is that he does not develop his idea but, quite the contrary, sidesteps it. The impersonal tone of this beginning reproduces, at the level of enunciation, the theme of the essay. The discourse then continues in the same affirmative and paratactic mode. The simple juxtaposition of assertions, together with the multiplication of words marking the impersonal ("every," "any," "there is") and of generalities, tends to obliterate the very existence of the person speaking and bring about an initial destabilization–a shaking or, as Emerson says, reawakening–of the listener or reader. Then, bit by bit, a scheme is introduced whereby the speaker is incarnated and the conditions of a sharing of the word are created: the "I," "our" and "we" in the third paragraph, certainly dependent on the conventions of enunciative abstraction characteristic of the philosophical style, yet good for bringing the discourse down to earth. Finally there is the sudden intrusion of a "you," which further implicates the reader. Now engaged, the reader is immediately, burningly addressed in the imperative: "*Stand* before each of its tablets and *say*, 'Under this mask did my Proteus nature hide itself.'" Implicated, made to take sides even as to the suggested order in which to pronounce a confession partaking of a magic formula, a "sesame" opening the door of his

---

[178] Emerson 1983, 237-41. Page numbers in parentheses, unless otherwise specified, refer to this edition (*Essays and Lectures*).

profound nature, the reader is cornered and is gratified with the promise of a remedy, a cure for the ill supposedly hindering his own growth: "This remedies the defect of our too great nearness to ourselves."

Thus this essay, begun under the sign of the impersonal, ends up inscribing its perspective in that of personal accomplishment, of intimate transformation. In the course of these first three paragraphs, Emerson's prose manages to envelop the reader in his own written outcome, capturing the listeners necessary to follow the essay and to accomplish the work of transformation which is its aim. Thus the beginning of "History"–the opening of the entire series of essays in Emerson's book–establishes the three modes of disjunction (the initial shake, the creation of the necessary pulling back of oneself), injunction (the imperative and exhortative forms), and conjunction (establishing a community of enunciation and the promise of a return to one's self).

These three modes continue to govern the rhythm of the rest of the essay, where they mingle and relay each other in multiple forms, in a hypnotic verbal choreography. Thus, the following page (239) establishes a whole rhetoric of sharing (with, for example, "we sympathize" and "..*for us,* as we ourselves in that place would have done...," and "We have the same interest in condition and character"). It punctuates this rhetoric of sharing and makes it dynamic with affirmations and injunctions ("...let us use in broad day," "The student is to read history actively and not passively," "The world exists for the education of each man," "there is no age or state of society..."), upheld by a whole thematic of moral perfectionism ("his unattained and attainable self"–disjunction/conjunction) and of the permanent exultation of human grandeur–of man in the present, who must always free himself from the phantoms of the past and from tradition (disjunctive mode). These three modes of Emersonian discourse operate as much in the order of discourse (its themes) as in that of the text (its functioning), and this synergy between philosophy and rhetoric provides the electric force of these spoken words: Emerson isn't satisfied with *saying* what he wants to say, he *produces* it, through a word which is an act/ active/enacted, agreeably to the philosophy he expounded in "The Poet": "Words and deeds are quite indifferent modes of the divine energy. Words are also actions, and actions are a kind of words" (450).

On the following page, as if to cut short the infinite possibilities of extending a paragraph governed by a logic of accumulation, Emerson declares abruptly: "I will not make more account of them. I believe in Eternity." (240). With this new clap of thunder, the speaker both validates his enunciation and holds it at a distance. These two sentences, paratactically juxtaposed in an electric cross-current of disjunctive and conjunctive modes, define the ultimate nature of the Emersonian essay as a discourse of faith.

Put to rout by "Eternity," History is consigned to dissolution. This dissolution is accomplished in the following paragraph, through a categorical affirmation operating in the disjunctive mode, since it practically annihilates the announced theme of the essay: "there is properly no history; only biography" (240). In all logic, this step to the side precedes an exhortation ("Every mind must know the whole lesson for itself,–must go over the whole ground"), this injunctive mode being confirmed by other "musts" and perfected by an imperative: "So stand before every public and private work..." (240-41). This decentering or displacement of the stuff of history, from the past toward the present–even its replacement, biography–is the principal motive of this essay's argumentation, and more broadly, one of the major themes of Emerson's thought, following from the famous opening paragraph of *Nature*, where it is nature that replaces history. Displacing history, making fun of it, suggesting its end by every means, smacks of millenarian thinking which, as we shall see, deeply characterizes Emerson's thought.

* * * * *

Although we could continue this way of analyzing the rhetoric of Emerson's essay, I will simply focus here on his two concluding pages. Emerson begins by emphasizing the act of closure: "I will not now go behind the general statement to explore the reason of this correspondency. Let it suffice that in the light of these two facts, namely that the mind is One, and that nature is its correlative, history is to be read and written" (255). In the next paragraph he draws all the "practical" consequences of this affirmation, dominated by the idea of the glorious future promised to man thus liberated from the phantoms of the past by the depth of experience. So everything seems to finish in the best way possible–the speaker is satisfied with the force of his exposition, and the reader delighted with such a promise–when all of a sudden, in a final decentering of the writing, the speaker, appearing to question himself, proclaims impudently: "Is there somewhat overweening in this claim? Then I reject all I have written, for what is the use of pretending to know what we know not?" (255) Boasting or facetious, the speaker manages a final destabilization of his discourse, this time going so far as to include himself in the disjunctive distancing from history. It is as if the essay, nearing its end, and threatened with becoming history in its turn, had to erase its own trace in order to be faithful to itself, suggesting that it too can become more than a vain tradition, only by finding its sense in the work of judgment and appropriation that it calls upon the reader to make. Note that this is not a matter of appropriating a content, a knowledge, but of suspending all knowing. Nothing is sure, nothing should be sure, and especially not something known: "I hold our actual knowledge very cheap" (256). Emerson thus intends a transcendence of the spoken word and of writing, and forestalls any fossilization of the written, any process of identification, any reverence. It is a clever strategy meant to win the reader's approval by playing the comedy of weakness and ignorance. This about-face shows with what complexity rhetoric can achieve the disjunctive mode, which revives the engendering power of discourse–"every ultimate fact is only the first of a new series" (405). Actually the disjunctive mode always appears in Emerson not as an abyss where hope is engulfed, but as the prelude to a re-founding, to a promise that supports a steadfast faith in the capacities of man, provided he will consent to what Emerson calls "an ethical reformation" (256): "Already that day exists for us, shines in on us at unawares, but the path of science and of letters is not the way into nature. The idiot, the Indian, the child and unschooled farmer's boy, stand nearer to the light by which nature is to be read, than the dissector or the antiquary" (256). It is consistent with the deep logic of this essay that it should conclude with this romantic exaltation of so-called "primitive" beings–precisely, situated as if outside *history*– whose supposed ignorance is compensated by the fact that the divine light guides and enlightens them. They are, because of this, closer to the universal, which Emerson calls upon us to experience. Unquestionably this concluding sentence of "History," having become the cornerstone of the Emersonian canon, aims above all at provoking the reader. It is an apparently paradoxical affirmation which seems at first to exclude us. It nevertheless lets us glimpse–and invites us to call our own–the possibility of a redemption whose only price is a conversion of an ethical order.

The analysis of "History" has brought out certain essential traits of the rhetoric of the Emersonian essay. I would now like to show how Emerson's rhetoric is connected more broadly to his esthetics. In the course of the preceding analysis, we saw that the Emersonian practice of literature was dictated by an ethical aim, an aim that Emerson assigned in fact to all esthetic practice in "Art," the essay which concludes the *Essays: First Series*.

The Notion of Literary Ethics

The notion of literary ethics seems particularly well suited to a discussion of the Emersonian practice of literature.

Although chosen by Emerson as the title of an essay ("Literary Ethics," 1838), this essential Emersonian notion is never really defined in his work. Indeed Emerson viewed literature–and, more generally, art–as an ethical enterprise, not a strictly esthetic one: "The use of literature is to afford us a platform whence we may command a view of our present life, a purchase by which we may move it" (408). It was in no case considered as an activity in and of itself, but as the agent of a knowledge and transformation involving the imperative toward moral perfection. With deep roots in the traditions of the sermon and of Puritan meditation, the spoken text never has meaning except in relation to something beyond itself: it can offer moral advancement or spiritual comfort, but not the material satisfaction of the pleasure of the text as such. Emerson never stops circumscribing the meaning of art in the idea of teaching, advice-giving or exhortation, of liberation. Thus, he declares in "Art," "Art has not yet come to its maturity, if it do not put itself abreast of the most potent influences of the world, if it is not practical and moral, if it do not stand in connection with the conscience, if it do not make the poor and uncultivated feel that it addresses them with a voice of lofty cheer" (437). In a sense, this ethical aim also situates the Emersonian essay in the tradition of the ancient moralists. The point of the essay is to counsel and recommend, to illuminate and guide action. Thus one finds in "Literary Ethics" for example an entire language of counsel and exhortation: "admonished," "enjoining," supported by faith that "Nature... is one and perfect." If, in this spirit, the injunctive mode predominates ("Explore, and explore"), the insistence on conceiving life as "exploration," "experience," "perpetual inquiry" exalts disjunction and removes all risk of rigid direction of conscience, to the extent that it invites each person to incline toward self-fulfillment–"our life is an apprenticeship to the truth" (403). A cardinal tenet of the transcendentalist movement, the idea of a divinity in man is the guarantee of all human freedom. This perspective clearly negates the autonomy of the esthetic, considered only for its power to transform individuals.

Literature as Experience

If life must be experience, literature itself, in a relationship of exemplification, appears as experience. Emerson emphasizes this idea on many occasions in his *Essays* (a term which indicates the genre's experimental character). Writing always appears as an exercise, a method, a mode of self-exploration, the promise of revelation and moral development. Conscience, Emerson never ceases to remind us, is always a process, and writing essays is related to the "spiritual exercises" of ancient philosophy or to Puritan meditation. The very nature of the Emersonian composition–where the concept takes form successively, first in the journals, then the lecture and finally the essay–stresses the dynamic character of the thought and the transitory nature of the essay, a mere step toward the accomplishment of something which transcends it, the appropriation of its power by the reader–"and that which builds is better than that which is built" ("Circles," 404). In this perspective, Emerson keeps underlining the role of art as a process rather than a product: "Our best praise is given to what [the arts] aimed and promised, not to the actual result," he declares in "Art" (437). Never should the movement of being stand still or be confused with a formula; neither should the essay ever be taken for an end in itself. As he states in his journal: "[I do not wish to] bring men to me but to themselves. I delight in driving them from me."[179] And in "Art," in a disjunctive movement abruptly discrediting the essay's presumed subject, Emerson exclaims, as in "History": "Away with your nonsense of oil and easels, of marble and chisels: except to open your eyes to the masteries of eternal art, they are hypocritical rubbish" (434). The sole aim of this provocative expression is to prevent the reader from ever entering into the comfort of a discourse. Art is true when it gains its force on either side of

---

[179] Emerson 1978, 258.

itself: "The reference of all production at last to an aboriginal Power explains the traits common to all works of the highest art,–that they are universally intelligible; that they restore us to the simplest states of mind; and are *religious*" (434; my emphasis). Art has legitimacy only in its capacity to restore to us a primal closeness with the world, to make it more intelligible to us, simpler, beyond the accumulation and sediment which seem to make it more familiar, more human, but in fact only complicate our relationship with it. This art which touches on the most fundamental aspects of the world and man, supremely ethical, raises itself to the religious level, as the subsequent paragraphs of the essay show: the speaker, placing his own experience at the heart of the discourse, inserts micro-stories and mini-sermons in the double form of addresses to himself and exhortations to the reader, in which he assigns an essential and highly symbolic place to Raphael's *Transfiguration*.

Beyond Art

However, Emerson never allows us a firm point of anchorage. As we would expect from now on, the conjunctive movement sketched earlier is immediately counterbalanced by a disjunctive dodge: "Yet when we have said all our fine things about the arts, we must end with a frank confession, that the arts, as we know them, are but initial" (437). A prime word of this concluding essay, "initial" gains value from the intimacy that is invoked between speaker and reader. The gentle irony of "when we have all said all our fine things about the arts" not only introduces a distance between the speaker and the object of his statement, but also, almost taking the form of free indirect discourse, subtly involves the reader in an exchange–once again, the participative rhetoric that is characteristic of the Emersonian essay. Thus emphasized, this paragraph then develops the essential idea of the essay, and a key element of Emerson's thought–that of transcending art, and of the revolutionary value of this transcendence. Indeed it is not just a matter of vilifying the arts in terms reminiscent of Plato's criticism and the iconoclastic enthusiasm of Puritan forebears, but of proposing a new sense of art: "Art should exhilarate, and throw down the walls of circumstance on every side, awakening in the beholder the same sense of universal relation and power which the work evinced in the artist, and its highest effect is to make new artists" (437). And this is the point: to make each of us an artist. With this call, Emerson offers the esthetic version of that democratic ideal identified with the evolution of America. Such is the highest destiny of art for Emerson, and he affirms it to be within the reach of any truly ethical existence.

Recognizing in each person an authentic power of creation, Emerson summons us to a veritable art of living: "Life may be lyric or epic, as well as a poem or romance," he declares (438). Ultimately we should tear down the partitions and put an end to "the separate existence of art" (438). In other words the renewal of art, its true accomplishing, would be identical to its disappearance in its historical form. On the other hand, it would be the duty of each person to make himself the creator of his own world ("Build, therefore, your own world"[180]) and of his own sovereign existence as an individual in a democratic society, not in the esthetic mode–Emerson remains vigorously opposed to all form of estheticism (439)–but in that of an ethics freed from any mere identification with moral rules. Each person is thus called upon to sculpt his own statue, to become at every instant the interpreter of his own existence, in a perpetual improvisation: "All works of art should not be detached, but extempore performances. A great man is a new statue in every attitude and action" (438). Art must vanish, must yield before life. Thus the new esthetic paradigm is not music, the frivolous refinement of the oratorio, but indeed the voice, the living voice, the simple and democratic instrument by which we may hear the concert of existence interpreted by every individual. Seeking to affirm the humanity in everyone, Emerson refuses both the estheticism of

---

[180] "Nature," Emerson 1983, 48

any existence not wholly ethical, and any esthetics resembling a flight from reality, "an asylum from the evils of life" (439). Esthetics must be not a search for pleasure but a religious experience: "As soon as beauty is sought, not from religion and love, but for pleasure, it degrades the seeker" (439). Emerson here draws upon the classical opposition between *eros* and *agape*.[181] In Emerson's eyes, every work of art is guilty of never doing enough to escape from estheticism. Hence the critical intransigence found throughout all his writings; no work can find total and enduring favor in his eyes. Hence too, in the Emersonian essay, a writing strategy that designates an external realm of meaning. This is the purport of Emerson's suspicion of the book in "The American Scholar":

> Books are the best of things, well used: abused, among the worst. What is the right use? What is the one end, which all means go to effect? They are for nothing but to inspire. I had better never see a book, than to be warped by its attraction clean out of my own orbit, and made a satellite instead of a system. The one thing in the world, of value, is the active soul. This every man is entitled to; this every man contains within him, although, in almost all men, obstructed, and as yet unborn. (57)

Emerson, as a good Protestant, shifts the authority of the book toward the voice which creates it–hence his transcendence of the text, hence too his emphasis on declarative devices through his essays and speeches. It becomes clear why Emerson considered the voice superior to the oratorio. I would even suggest that this constant effort to transcend literature actually means that there is no possible deepening of Emerson's thought by repeated reading; rather, the essay is there to abrade and

---

[181] I.e., desire versus selfless love. See also p. 118, footnote (Ed.)

destabilize. That is its only function and we come back to it for more abrasion of surfaces, not for a better understanding. What matters is the power of literature "to unsettle all things" ("Circles," 412), "the power of poetry to unfix" ("History," 251).

Esthetics, Ethics and Religion–A Fusion

Such a conception of literature is indissociable from the democratic ideal. For Emerson this is a political ideal, not reform or social criticism. He is not prescriptive, but affirms the utopian value of art, its liberating power: "Poets are thus liberating gods" ("The Poet," 461-62). This art which is a necessity and a promise opens the path to a new life, or simply to life. Art need no longer lead a separate and vain existence, but, ascending to the highest end of humanity ("[Art] must begin farther back in man," 439), would serve to bring forth a new Adam. "It would be better to begin higher up" (439). This transcendence of art is in fact a beginning, a new beginning, going back to the original man, who is but the symbol of the original man still alive deep inside us. As a good moralist Emerson criticizes the derailment of the everyday by a mad, death-inflicting "art"–"[they] create a death which they call poetic" (439), and summons us to seek the beauty of the ordinary, which is illuminated by the "ideal" to be found "in the very act of drinking and eating, the fact of breathing, the vital functions" (439). And he adds: "Beauty must come back to the useful arts, and the distinctions between the fine and the useful arts be forgotten" (439). At its conclusion, "Art" could almost be an avant-garde manifesto of the twentieth century: Emerson expounds a functionalist conception of an art destined to a great future, from Frank Lloyd Wright and the Bauhaus to industrial design. He creates a radical displacement of esthetic activity–no longer a specialized practice, it becomes everyone's business, in an affirmation of the genius of every individual. Separating art from its institutional allegiances is another way to create democratic man, who Emerson thought would be marvelously represented by the American.

Abolishing any separate realm of art means designing an ethical project in which the individual is reborn unto himself, and a political project in which the sense of community is redefined. Through his *Essays*, Emerson thus accomplished the mission of the intellectual whose role, in a democratic society, is to reveal to each person that his potential is equal to that of any other, and to guide him in his efforts toward moral and spiritual elevation. Emerson's concern with power and potentiality throughout his writings amply illustrates how much his discourse affirms individual strength against power, against all powers. Emerson's style itself seems an example of how he sees esthetics as ethics, and represents his call for a democratic esthetics: his essays are as devoid of hierarchical principle as the democratic ideal he invokes.

* * * * *

We have seen that esthetics' lack of autonomy has as a consequence or corollary the permanent transcendence of literature that is at the heart of Emersonian discourse. On account of his ethical goal of individual self-reform, and on account of the political perspective that this reform opens in a democratic society, esthetics always seems to concern something beyond itself. I would suggest that the ultimate goal of Emerson's work is a fusion of the esthetic, ethical, and religious spheres–akin to the one his contemporary Søren Kierkegaard also sought.

A Sketch of Emersonian Millenarism

The corollary of the Emersonian idea of an art of life is the death of art, the end of art: art exists only as an ethical project and, in a way, only realizes itself in abolishing itself– when it fulfills itself in each of us and contributes to the re-establishment of society. This end of art, which is not simply metaphoric, is, like the end of history, transcended and abolished. Such an idea partakes of millenarist thinking, Emerson's heritage from the Second Great Awakening, the evangelical renewal between 1800 and 1830 which postulated the coming, beyond history, of the Kingdom of Heaven described in the Apocalypse–a kingdom perfectly incarnating conjunction.[182]

Indeed, as we have seen, one of the essential movements of Emerson's thought tends toward the transcendence of history, in two specific forms. In the first, history is transcended by human nature. In the essay "History," Emerson claims a double displacement of history, from the past toward the present, and from the external (the world, society) toward the internal (the individual, the mind), by which biography replaces history. The individual must appropriate all history: this is possible because he has in himself all the virtualities of human nature, therefore the capacity to feel all past events, good or bad. In the second, history is transcended by nature in the sense of the physical world. It is significant that the essay "History" devotes a considerable amount of space to nature, and that the essay "Nature" grants an important place to history.

America, as is well known, was founded on the dream of transcending history, left behind in old Europe, and of a new departure, a new beginning of human history in an America identified with nature. To the extent that he celebrates nature, Emerson thus presents himself as a regenerator of the American project: America has forgotten that it was built on a utopia, and Emerson fully undertakes to remind her of her promise.

Just as he often adopts the perspective of history's end, Emerson in "Art" raises the question of the goal of art. Indeed, the ultimate and radical accomplishment of any true esthetic project seems to be the formation of a community of creators–"its highest effect is to make new artists" (437)–which is established beyond time and space:

---

[182] Robinson (21-22) signals the importance of this millenarist heritage in what is nowadays known as Emerson's "optimism."

When the thought of Plato becomes a thought to me, – when a truth that fired the soul of Pindar fires mine, time is no more. When I feel that we two meet in a perception, that our two souls are tinged with the same hue, and do, as it were, run into one, why should I measure degrees of latitude, why should I count Egyptian years? (249)

The millenarist nature of this vision–a kingdom peopled with a community of creators–stems notably from the fact that Emerson seems never to envisage the idea that this faithfulness to one's self which conditions the art of living free of all restrictions could give rise to a penchant for evil or indeed for insignificance. The individual is presumed good, guided by faith and unscathed by any corruption of intent.

Redemption by the Word

Emersonian discourse is thus defined by the redeeming value of word and writing, in the sense that it restores man's ultimate possibilities and identifies their achievement with the coming of a promised kingdom. This major dimension of Emerson's rhetoric is inseparable from his concept of the poet as a redeemer with a sacramental function, as defined in "The Poet" or in one of his less known works, "Thoughts on Modern Literature." All his rhetoric rests on the idea that the spoken word is capable of stimulating the reader's awareness, of awakening him to a process of self-knowledge: it is a "spiritual exercise" which does not aim for a knowledge or a reflection on knowledge, but the transformation of the other person, of the reader or listener–it is a word of conversion, a word of redemption, a word of deliverance. To this logic of discourse there corresponds a logic not of argumentation but of the text, a movement of thought and word which is supposed to produce a revelation in the reader and bring him to share a belief. Emerson does not intend that the reader absorb a knowledge or a doctrine, but instead the movement of discovery and self-transformation (which corresponds to the movement of thought into action). Emerson's writings seem destined to inspire, to communicate to the reader, by contagion, a confidence in oneself (and in America).

High priest of the possible, of hope, of the Ideal, Emerson imparts to his word a religious dimension, which he feels is at the heart of all veritable art. Thus he criticizes Goethe, in "Thoughts on Modern Literature": "Goethe, then, must be set down as the poet of the Actual, not of the Ideal; the poet of limitation, not of possibility; of this world, and not of religion and hope; in short, if I may say so, the poet of prose, and not of poetry" (1165). Emerson—an apostle of participative writing in which author and reader join one another in celebrating not only the real but also the possible which haunts him, advocating the sovereignty of an *I* which is only the other side of the Divine—always remained a profoundly religious spirit. Every page, and virtually every paragraph, bears witness to this. As further proof of the continuity between Emerson the pastor and Emerson the lecturer and essayist, consider these lines of a sermon delivered on October 3, 1830, in which Emerson evoked for the first time his notion of "self-reliance" in terms which very closely prefigure his essay of that title (1841):

> Nor, on the other hand, let it be thought that there is in this self-reliance anything of presumption, anything inconsistent with the spirit of dependence and piety toward God. In listening more intently to our own soul we are not becoming in the ordinary sense more selfish, but are departing farther from what is low and falling back upon truth and upon God. For the whole value of the soul depends on the fact that it contains a divine principle, that it is a house of

God, and the voice of the eternal inhabitant may always be heard within it.[183]

Literature and, more generally, artistic creation, was for Emerson an enterprise of an ethical nature, whose aim is not a knowledge, nor a reflection on knowledge, but an invitation to self-transformation and action. Far from being an ideal expressed only conceptually, this idea is put into practice through the construction of a close relationship between speaker and reader, the construction of a stage whereon different systems of discourse together effect a veritable rhetoric of provocation. Based on a defiance of all estheticism and always pointing beyond literature, Emerson's literary ethics place him in the lineage of the sermon and demonstrate the pervasive influence of millenarist thinking.

---

[183] Emerson 2001, 16-17.

7

Emerson's Rhetoric of Empowerment: "Address on the Fugitive Slave Law"

As a writer, Emerson fundamentally envisioned his mission as the individual moral transformation of his fellow Americans. The urgency of this mission seemed all the more pressing when he publicly lent his support to the growing antislavery movement. More than ever, from 1844 onward, certain of his writings purported to have a transforming power. To that end Emerson arrayed all the rhetorical and metaphorical resources of language. Emerson's strategy becomes clear through a close reading of a passage from his "Address to the Citizens of Concord on the Fugitive Slave Law," delivered at Concord, Massachusetts, on May 3, 1851:

> One intellectual benefit we owe to the late disgraces. The crisis had the illuminating power of a sheet of lightning at midnight. It showed truth. It ended a good deal of nonsense we had been wont to hear and to repeat, on the 19th April, the 17th June, and the 4th July. It showed the slightness and unreliableness of our social fabric; it showed what stuff reputations are made of; what straws we dignify by office and title, and how competent we are to give counsel and help in a day of trial. It showed the shallowness of leaders; the divergence of parties from their alleged grounds; showed that men would not stick to what they had said: that the resolution of

public bodies, or the pledges never so often given and put on record of public men, will not bind them. The fact comes out more plainly, that you cannot rely on any man for the defence of truth, who is not constitutionally, or by blood and temperament, on that side. A man of a greedy and unscrupulous selfishness may maintain morals when they are in fashion: but he will not stick. However close Mr. Wolf's nails have been pared, however neatly he has been shaved, and tailored, and set up on end, and taught to say "Virtue and Religion," he cannot be relied on at a pinch: he will say, morality means pricking a vein. The popular assumption that all men loved freedom, and believed in the Christian religion, was found hollow American brag. Only persons who were known and tried benefactors are found standing for freedom: the sentimentalists went down stream. I question the value of our civilization, when I see that the public mind had never less hold of the strongest of all truths. The sense of injustice is blunted,–a sure sign of the shallowness of our intellect. I cannot accept the railroad and telegraph in exchange for reason and charity. It is not skill in iron locomotives that marks so fine civility as the jealousy of liberty. I cannot think the most judicious tubing a compensation for metaphysical debility. What is the use of admirable law-forms and political forms, if a hurricane of party feeling and a combination of monied interests can beat them to the ground? What is the use of courts, if judges only quote authorities, and no judge exerts original jurisdiction, or recurs to first principles? What is the use of a Federal Bench, if its opinions are the

political breath of the hour? And what is the use
of constitutions, if all the guaranties provided by
the jealousy of the ages for the protection of
liberty are made of no effect, when a bad act of
Congress finds a willing commissioner?[184]

Emerson's Address is one of the most famous political
speeches denouncing the Fugitive Slave Law of September 1850.
As part of a larger deal known as the Compromise of 1850
(which was meant to accommodate Southern slaveholders in
order to preserve the Union), the Fugitive Slave Law required
the Northern states to assist in the recapture of runaway slaves.
Ever since the abolition of slavery in some New England states
in the aftermath of the American Revolution, fugitive slaves had
repeatedly escaped from their condition in the slave states to take
refuge in the North. Emerson was urged to deliver this address
after two notorious attempts to recapture fugitive slaves in
Boston[185] had heightened public awareness that this law
supported the spread of slavery and compromised the perceived
moral integrity of the North.

Although the Address belongs to a lesser-known part of
the Emerson corpus–which has come under sustained scrutiny
only recently[186]–it is of great interest as a record of his
involvement in public affairs when faced with the heated debate
over slavery in the United States of the 1850s. After voicing his
sense of historical crisis, Emerson describes what he perceives as
its two sources–the overriding materialism of Northern society,

---

[184] Emerson 1995, 55-56.

[185] The capture of Shadrach Minkins in February 1851 and that of
Thomas Sims in April of that year had met with dramatic organized
resistance, spearheaded by Boston activists and abolitionists of both
races. In an effective blow to the Fugitive Slave Law, Minkins was
rescued from the Boston courthouse and spirited away to freedom.
The abolitionists' attempted rescue of Sims was foiled by better-
organized official forces. (Ed.)

[186] Cf. esp. Gougeon, Collison, and Gonnaud.

conducive to misguided party politics, on the one hand, and the weakening of moral authorities (religion and courts), on the other hand. At the same time, the moral stance on which he grounds his argument underlines the role of the individual as the only source of legitimate authority and as the proving-ground of democracy, thus providing the rationale for the call to civil disobedience which is the ultimate goal of the Address.

The beginning of the paragraph under consideration voices Emerson's sense of historical crisis, which he likens to a thunderstorm–an idea echoed further down in his reference to "a hurricane." But one should note that he chooses to concentrate on one aspect of thunderstorms, namely "a sheet of lightning" and its "illuminating power." What it illuminates is the moral hypocrisy in which America has wallowed for so long. Emerson stresses the contrast between the "popular assumptions" about the identity and values of New England, as self-proclaimed birthplace of the Republic and symbol of America's commitment to freedom, on the one hand, and its complicity in the growing power of the slaveholding states during the 1850s, on the other. That equation of America with freedom is symbolized by the historic dates enumerated at the beginning of the passage, which are milestones in the American Revolution: the 19th of April and the 17th of June are the famous battles in Concord and Boston respectively in 1775, while of course the Fourth of July saw the adoption of the Declaration of Independence in 1776. Emerson treats these symbols ironically, going so far as to call their annual commemorations "nonsense," thus questioning the accepted truths about America's history and exposing the fundamental hypocrisy of American society. The main message of Emerson's Address is that although the United States has achieved political independence from its mother country, it remains dependent upon the moral evil of slavery, which annihilates the validity of such self-descriptions as "the land of freedom."

What he particularly aims at here are the notions of custom ("wont to") and uncritical repetition ("to repeat"): the commemoration of America's founding events has become a mere celebration of dates, rather than a reminder of the exacting and continuing fight for freedom. In other words America has become tradition instead of process, and if it is evolving at all, Emerson charts the downward spiral of an American republic and democracy entangled in the moral evil of slavery.

The revelatory power of the crisis is thus to expose a fundamental weakness in the process of nation-making, namely "the slightness and unreliableness of our social fabric": "fabric" means "frame" or "structure," and in this sense it partakes of the "house divided" metaphor inherited from the New Testament (Mark 3:25) and famously illustrated by Abraham Lincoln in a speech of 1858, in which he uses it to describe the division between the North and the South. But fabric is also cloth, so that the phrase vividly conveys the idea of the tearing process affecting the United States. The sense of disruption conveyed both by the images of the "sheet of lightning" and the more pervasive notion of the tearing (or tearing down) of the "social fabric" show how much the Compromise of 1850 seemed to have undermined the promise of America. Confronted with such a sense of crisis, Emerson feels urged to challenge a country that has negated itself.

In the sense of cloth, the term "fabric" is echoed in the word "stuff," which introduces a more focused consideration of the role played by particular groups of people in the present crisis. Emerson launches a virulent attack against "the shallowness of leaders," who are also characterized as "straws": a straw–or man of straw–is a person of no substance, whose acts appear to be controlled by others, like a puppet. Indeed, Emerson here vividly suggests the image of a rag doll-like man, which his use of "stuff" also brings to mind. Emerson's vocabulary evokes men who have ceased to be living creatures: the politician Webster, for one, had become an institution instead of a man, in the same way that America as a whole had become institutionalized.[187] Although Emerson does not mention Webster by name in this paragraph, his attack on "the shallowness of leaders" is more particularly aimed at the man whose support proved decisive in the passage of a law which incensed many Northerners–a move which Emerson had already named as "Mr. Webster's treachery" earlier in the Address. Emerson uses the resources of satire when he creates the image of "Mr. Wolf" (Webster again?), whose transformation into a respectable citizen and virtuous leader is only superficial, and whose true nature is revealed by a soulless enactment such as the Fugitive Slave Law.

Proslavery Politics and the Pursuit of Material Wealth

The second aspect of Emerson's assessment of the political situation in the early 1850s is his denunciation of party politics and the materialism of American society.

Indeed, if men are shallow, it is because they are not themselves, that is "true men," but are in thrall to the workings of party politics, which have become void of any moral substance: Emerson stresses "the divergence of parties from their alleged grounds," in other words their inconsistency and hypocrisy. Both in his writings and his life, Emerson had always evinced a strong distrust of party politics–which accounted for his reluctance to join regular abolitionist organizations, in spite of his increasingly radical commitment to their objectives, of which the Address is proof–and he was all the more incensed by a blatant form of political expediency such as the Fugitive Slave Law.

Next, Emerson pursues his indictment of the moral and political crisis with a sweeping denunciation of materialism, blaming in a single clause "a hurricane of party feeling and a combination of monied interests." If political parties shift "from

---

[187] Daniel Webster (1782-1852), a senator from Massachusetts and one of the foremost politicians of antebellum America, was one of the authors of the Compromise of 1850 and its Fugitive Slave Act.

their alleged grounds," it is because they are bound, not to their "resolutions" and "pledges," but to the economic power of the market economy. The ground for such deleterious acts as the Fugitive Slave Law was thus a pervasive materialism, which Emerson condemns here as stridently as in his earlier writings, going as far as to declare: "I question the value of our civilization..." Emerson's critique of the role played by Massachusetts in the crisis over the Fugitive Slave Law focuses on its leaders' appetite for material wealth and economic prosperity at the expense of moral standards and spiritual values (truth, justice, freedom, reason, and charity are all named). Emerson's attitude here is characteristic of a period in which "Things are in the saddle/And ride mankind," as he famously declared in verse at the time.[188] Further, when he declares, "I cannot accept the railroad in exchange for reason and charity," etc., Emerson offers a powerful critique of the rampant materialism of mid-nineteenth century society, which is bound to threaten, to compromise, the promise of America.

Emerson thus questions the value of a civilization in which conscience and moral integrity have been replaced by technological feats as the standard by which national achievement is to be assessed. He has in mind the various constituents of Webster's who supported the Fugitive Slave Law, and rebukes the philistine property-owning class symbolized in the "Cotton Whigs," the capitalist mill owners in such New England towns as Lowell, Massachusetts, whose complicity in the slave system derived from their dependence on the South's raw cotton for their textile production. What Emerson condemns is the empiricism and relativism of men like Webster, who prefer to listen to the voice of "monied interests" rather than to that of their own conscience, and who advance the reign of materialism instead of that of "reason and charity," two important words in the Address. In fact, the authors of the Fugitive Slave Act and those who supported its implementation grounded their action on

---

[188] "Ode, Inscribed to W. H. Channing," Emerson 2001, 445, lines 50-51.

"understanding" instead of "reason," and the famous distinction between Understanding and Reason inherited from Coleridge (who had borrowed it from Kantian philosophy) is pervasive in this passage. Broadly speaking, "understanding" characterizes the ordinary faculties of the mind as it is bent on organizing the world for purely practical and material purposes, whereas reason articulates mankind's affinity for spiritual truths and the moral law. "Understanding" brings merely a segmented–and in this context one may almost say "sectional"–view of the world, while "reason" is intent on the whole. In the same way his call to the Christian concept of "charity" or ideal love, which contrasts with the notion of "greedy and unscrupulous selfishness," indicates that for Emerson moral behavior should derive from religious principles, a necessity which is threatened by what he identifies as a growing lack of faith.[189]

The Collapse of Moral Authorities

Thus a third aspect of this text is Emerson's emphasis on the collapse of moral authorities. Emerson denounces not only the authors of the Fugitive Slave Act and the combination of political expediency and economic interests which led to its passage, but also the traditional bodies of authority in Massachusetts that have supported its implementation. He specifically mentions two: established religions and the courts, whose lack of faith and moral strength he forcefully denounces.

"The popular assumption that all men loved freedom, and believed in the Christian religion," he says, "was found hollow American brag." Religion has thus become as "hollow"

---

[189] "Charity" is the traditional translation of the Greek *agape*, most familiar in I Cor. 13:13: "And now abideth faith, hope, charity, these three: but the greatest of these is charity." The key text throwing light on this aspect of the text's rhetoric is "Worship," in which Emerson also associates a denunciation of materialism and the complicity of established religion with "the propagandism of slavery" (Emerson 1983, 1059).

as the political leaders are "shallow," a sure measure of how far America is losing its substance through lack of spiritual authenticity. Without "reason and charity," American society was bound to a "shallowness" and "hollowness" which in typically Emersonian fashion "mirrored" "the shallowness of our intellect." Emerson exposes what he elsewhere calls "the divorce between religion and morality" (in "Worship," published as an essay in 1860, but first delivered as a lecture on April 1, 1851[190]). Emerson particularly rebukes both Webster and the churches for lacking "reason" and failing to be consistent with the doctrines they preach. In a rhetoric which revives the harsh criticism that he had notoriously leveled at the Unitarian Church in his "Divinity School Address" of 1838, Emerson condemns the dead forms of a Christianity that has boiled down to nothing but complicity with the established powers. Instead of preaching "charity" (that is, ideal love paving the way for a millennial "nation of men... inspired by the Divine Soul," as he said in 1837 in "The American Scholar"[191]), the churches have surrendered to misguided politics, while political leaders have used religious discourse as a cover-up for the amorality of their politics of compromise.

In this Address Emerson also expresses contempt for the courts and a compliant federal government, whose legal decisions helped to strengthen the slave power. His audience would have known about the man who, like Webster, is the implicit villain here: Judge Lemuel Shaw, Chief Justice of the Massachusetts Supreme Judicial Court, who supported the Fugitive Slave Law. If the churches no longer foster reliance on the very principles that they should defend, the courts are evidently dominated by a sense of moral expediency or "prudence" which is at heart irreconcilable with a belief in democratic "first principles." In other words the courts and the judges, in their desire to implement human laws divorced from

---

[190] Emerson 1983, 1058.
[191] Emerson 1983, 71.

"spiritual laws,"[192] have become entangled in a misguided respect for "authorities," instead of exerting "original jurisdiction" or recurring to "first principles." This is a key notion, whose fundamental importance here is that it simultaneously characterizes what judges lacked, and defines the ultimate resource against moral blindness and the failings of organized bodies.

Redemptive Individualism and the New Nation

The fourth and last section of this commentary, therefore, will reconsider our Emerson passage from the viewpoint of the only valid alternative implied in it: the necessity for self-reliance (the individual as ultimate source of moral authority) and the redemptive power of individualism in the construction of a new nation (the individual as proving-ground of democracy).

If the various institutions–political parties and their leaders, the churches, the courts–have fallen into misguided action, then the individual alone appears to have the power to reverse the downward course of American history, and Emerson insists on the right and necessity of personal judgment in the face of orthodoxy and authority. The key term here is "first principles," a notion central to Emersonian transcendentalism, where it is synonymous with "higher law," a term Emerson also uses further on in this Address (363).

What is at work throughout this text is the fundamental difference between the common law of the courts–and even of the Constitution–and the higher law. For Emerson, as for Socrates or Thoreau,[193] one should obey an unwritten law superior to that of the state, and expressive of the permanent values of mankind, as opposed to "the political breath of the hour." This was a central argument in abolitionist speeches of the period, as testified for instance by Theodore Parker's

---

[192] See the essays "Prudence and "Spiritual Laws" in *Essays: First Series,* Emerson 1983.
[193] In "Civil Disobedience" (1849).

"Sermon on Conscience," delivered in September 1850, in which the abolitionist minister denounced those who "have forgotten that there is any law higher than the Constitution, any rights above vested rights."[194] In this speech Emerson appears to be on his way to joining radical abolitionists such as Parker and William Lloyd Garrison in their rejection of the value of the American Constitution, which proved unable to guarantee liberty in America: "what is the use of constitutions, if all the guaranties provided by the jealousy of ages for the protection of liberty are made of no effect...?"

Setting the resources of the self-reliant individual against the shortcomings of society, Emerson never ceased to trust the fundamental virtue and goodness of the individual, who appears as the only true resource against the evils of the state and of society. In this speech as in his earlier writings, Emerson argues in a Rousseauian way that evils come from institutions (political parties, churches, courts...) and not from individuals. Emerson thus intends his speech to empower the individual to act according to his true self and not to compromising politics. Since the individual's true self is construed as the universal self through the agency of natural laws, Emerson's appeal to individual self-reliance is intended to re-establish the threatened community.

The individual, the only true source of moral authority, is also the ultimate source of political legitimacy. Thus individualism does not run counter to community, but is the true prerequisite for its soundness, and Emerson's speech reminds us that the experiment of the American republic represented a relocation of absolute authority *within* rather than *outside* the self. Emerson refuses a democracy which requires the sacrifice of individual conscience in favor of a misguided sense of community, and puts forward self-reliance as the best ally of democracy.

---

[194] Delbanco 299.

Indeed Emerson delivered this Address not only to express his anger at "Webster's treachery" and the complicity of Massachusetts with the slaveholding powers, but in order to involve his audience in acts of civil disobedience, which he explicitly sanctions at the end of the Address: "This law must be made inoperative. It must be abrogated and wiped out of the statute book; but, while it stands there, it must be disobeyed."[195] What we see in this text is Emerson deliberately at work to free his audience from the shackles of a false respect for the law. Emerson's aim in this address is to instill or reinforce in his fellow citizens a sense of moral duty as opposed to blind obedience to an unjust law. Each individual is thus summoned to obey a "higher law" or "first principles," in a process of spiritual ascension which is meant to prefigure the sense of historical ascension which present politics had failed to embody.

Another American Jeremiad

The passage we have examined clearly situates Emerson's "Address to the Citizens of Concord on the Fugitive Slave Law" within the genre we considered in Chapter 2–the jeremiad, inherited from the Hebrew prophets and practiced by the 17th-century Puritans who were Emerson's spiritual forebears. This religious genre combined a lamentation over the present ills of the community (ascribed to a lack of faith and moral iniquities often involving materialism), and a subsequent call to repent and reform as a way to a renewed covenant with God and a brighter future.

As a former minister, Emerson knew this tradition perfectly, and it effectively informs the rhetorical strategy at work in this part of the Address–which Emerson eventually delivered ten times to various communities in Massachusetts. The jeremiad allowed Emerson simultaneously to denounce the evils of the time and to empower his audience (and future

---

[195] Emerson 1995, 71.

readers, since the speech would be widely circulated through the press) to resist what he perceived as an unjust and deleterious law. The Address is no philosophical disquisition or outlet for private concern, but an appeal to arms–peaceful arms as yet, to be sure, but destined to be more forceful several years later, with the rebellion of John Brown at Harpers Ferry and its defense by a few lone transcendentalists, notably Thoreau. This speech–Emerson's counterpart to Thoreau's "Civil Disobedience" (1849)–marks a turning point in Emerson's involvement in abolitionist politics. In 1851, however, Emerson's main thrust was still to appeal to the redeeming force of individual conscience, to the integrity of the individual against the artificial values of a society that makes compromises. Its objective was nonetheless as clear as it was morally binding, and Emerson put his convictions into practice through his support–along with like-minded residents of Concord–of the "Underground Railroad," the network of activists who lent assistance to fugitive slaves passing through Boston and Concord en route to Canada, there to find the freedom denied to them even in Massachusetts.

8

"Truth comes in with darkness": Transparence and Opacity in Melville's "Piazza"

Melville's Later Works: From the Divine to the Grotesque

In this and the following chapters, I consider aspects of transcendence expressed in some later works by another great figure of the "American Renaissance," Herman Melville. As is well known, the author of *Moby-Dick* did not share the transcendentalist idealism of such thinkers as Emerson and Thoreau. Melville's difficult quest for philosophic anchorage, powerfully pursued through the less well-known collection entitled *The Piazza Tales*, adds new dimensions to the evolving concept of transcendence.

I. Picturesque Delights

The first part of "The Piazza," the opening story of Melville's *Piazza Tales*, is entirely oriented toward a celebration of the delights of picturesque nature, the narrator inviting us to share his exultation before the variety and the richness of the spectacle.[196] As the story begins, the narrator has moved to the

---

[196] I use "picturesque" to mean the contemplation of nature as a painting, according to the conventions of landscape painting, and not in the sense of an esthetic category halfway between the beautiful and the sublime. On the meaning of this term in classical esthetics, see notably Walter J. Hipple (1957).

countryside, effecting a retirement similar to that of Thoreau on the shore of Walden Pond. Melville's narrator has settled at the border between "country" nature and wild nature, enjoying a panoramic view of the latter from his house. Leaving behind the society of men, he seems devoted to the charming society of nature, which he begins to savor, he tells us, by sitting down on a "royal lounge of turf" (2), further echoing Thoreau's experience.

In "Where I Lived and What I Lived For," the second chapter of *Walden*, Thoreau invoked with enthusiasm the happy identity of the *seat* and the *site* where a man's home is located: "Wherever I sat, there I might live, and the landscape radiated from me accordingly. What is a house but a *sedes*, a seat?–better if a country seat. I discovered many a site for a house not likely to be soon improved..."[197]

Melville prolongs the echo of this dreamy etymology linking *seat/sit/site/side* throughout all this part of his narrative, especially in the long and facetious discussion on the orientation of his veranda. This piazza, or porch,[198] an improvement over the turf lounge that makes the contemplation of nature more enjoyable and marks a certain advance in his settling into the world, is endowed with a prime virtue, transparency, which also seems to echo the house at Walden: "With this more substantial shelter about me, I had made some progress toward settling in the world. This frame, so slightly clad, was a sort of crystallization around me, and reacted on the builder. It was suggestive somewhat as a picture in outlines."[199]

And when the narrator decides to orient his veranda toward the north, contrary to the advice of all the neighbors, this choice can only seem a kindly mockery of Thoreau, a parody intended to bring out the loony, rather than truly rebellious, character of his eccentricity. We may thus consider the narrator

---

[197] Thoreau 1971, 81.

[198] The roofed porch generally called a *veranda(h)* is also styled *piazza* in New England and the Southern Atlantic states, and *gallery* in the South. (Ed.)

[199] Thoreau 1971, 85.

in the first part of "The Piazza" as Melville's caricature of Thoreau.[200]

Now settled on his veranda, Melville's narrator can bask in a nature which appears entirely as a refuge, a haven of peace, and the site of meaning. Viewed–structured–according to traditional 18th-century esthetic conceptions, nature becomes landscape, and it is this transparent equivalence of nature and art that building a veranda must celebrate. In his constructing a veranda, he is the architect not so much of a structure than of the spectacle it will afford him: he validates this "prospect" (2)[201] created by his judicious choice of location. Offering the ideal place for contemplation, the veranda assures the narrator's settled comfort as he contemplates a perspective of which he is master and beneficiary. The short story radicalizes and dramatizes the keenly felt esthetic dimension which characterizes the picturesque vision and conditions the narrator's relationship to the world.

As an avatar of rationalism, the picturesque demonstrates a faith in the ability of reason to organize the world by means of conventions which are all based on perspective, whose principle and function are to frame what is seen and assign a place to objects according to optical rules–a mechanism to convert the world into an arrangement of *readable signs*. The perception of the landscape is itself only the virtual body, in the mind's eye, of a landscape painting based on the theory of perspective defined in the Renaissance–a theory, a mental construct whose keystone is that vanishing point which substitutes for infinity, and therefore, in a way, humanizes the

---

[200] "The Piazza" was written in January-February 1856, scarcely a year and a half after the publication of *Walden* (Aug. 9, 1854), which inspired Melville in part to compose two other short stories, "I and my Chimney" and "The Apple-Tree Table," between summer 1854 and autumn 1855, and alluding respectively to the "Housewarming" and "Conclusion" chapters of *Walden* (as Sealts shows [1988, 93]).

[201] Parenthetical page references are to *The Piazza Tales and Other Prose Pieces, 1839-60,* ed. H. Hayford et al. (Melville 1987).

absolute. It is a Promethean enterprise, this invention where the vanishing takes place not only in the depth of an abstract space, but at a far remove from the divine. As a distancing of the divine which, no longer the reason of the world, yields to mathematical ratio and is abruptly stripped of its medieval and Byzantine frontality, perspective defines the world by projection, thereby opening the way to the subjectivization of art which continues in our time.

Provided that the constructive procedures of linear perspective guarantee the uniform and coherent depth of the field of vision, and each aspect of nature is thus carefully organized by the will of a sovereign gaze, it seems that contemplation will bring an infallible serenity, rather like those *vedute* or "views" of an urban or a pastoral paradise which enjoyed great success in the 17th and 18th centuries.[202] This is a naïve illusion, to be sure, and the narrator's naïveté is what Melville seeks to disclose in the second part of his tale, by dissociating vision from meaning. It is clear indeed that this axis of perspective, vanishing toward the horizon and saturated with the transparency and the readability of the signs that it has to organize, is not that "very axis of reality" that Melville, like Shakespeare, had the ambition to probe.[203]

II. Substance and Signs

1. Rebellion of the sign

---

[202] Strictly, the *veduta* usually designates an urban landscape painting. More broadly, it can refer to the whole tradition of creating ideal views, from landscape painting to the art of the garden.

[203] See Melville, "Hawthorne and his Mosses": "But it is those deep far-away things in him; those occasional flashings-forth of the intuitive Truth in him; those short, quick probings at the very axis of reality;–these are the things that make Shakespeare, Shakespeare" (Melville 1987, 244).

From the piazza, some uncertain object I had
caught, mysteriously snugged away, to all
appearance, in a sort of purple breast-pocket,
high up in a hopper-like hollow, or sunken
angle, among the northwestern mountains–yet,
whether, really, it was on a mountain-side, or a
mountain-top, could not be determined... (4)

Set in the convolutions of a visible space that was
supposed to be neatly organized by landscape's perspective, an
"uncertain object" appears, its rebellious power surpassing the
simple reserve of newness that space borrows from time. That
uncertainty makes it a scandalous object, whose scandal is
precisely that it is not sufficiently an object (while making an
object of the one who is looking and who sees himself looked
at), thus eluding all capture. Escaping from the objectivizing
claim of the gaze which organizes and enjoys the landscape, the
uncertain object causes the gaze to fail, makes it falter in the
fault where the object, a spot of light, is lodged.

Like a flaw in the landscape, like a rip in the theatrical
canvas hung before the veranda, this spot of light particularly
contradicts one of the archetypes of the picturesque, the infinite
regression of tone.[204] In a representational space traditionally
defined as concave–such as this "charmed ring" (1) of the
mountains–this spot of light, commandingly capturing the eye,
seems wholly extended toward the fore-plane of the canvas–a
gash of a powerful convexity, transgressive to the point of
touching the eye, in an *agon* in which the haptic triumphs over
the optic. Emerging from the wings, from behind the curtains of
a nature which was only the empty theatre of its own
(re)presentation, this light spilling forth does not form the
vanishing point of the landscape, but instead decenters and
dismembers it.

---

[204] As seen, notably, in the paintings of Claude Lorrain, the
seventeenth-century master of ideal-landscape painting.

The convolutions of the mountain are at once the site of its appearing and the concealment of its origin. Opposite the veranda, which seemed a place of salvation, the spot of light reveals a metaphysical unease: it captures the gaze which sought to be detached and self-sufficient, implicating it in its folds. It now occurs to the narrator that his true location cannot be the *sedes* or seat whence his gaze composes the landscape to his scale and contemplates it in its infinite temporal unfolding. Rather, it is this indefinite place, the refuge of immoderation and excess–this background that is the base and foundation, beyond the bounds of any well-regulated organization of the visible. This sign, however, does not signify an overabundance of being; it is the analog of a *voice* addressing him *indistinctly*–different from that "blue summit" which "will, as it were, talk to you ... and plainly tell you..." (4). Not a sensory overload, but rather a surge, ultimate and marginal, of the absolute. The mystery is this: that within the contingence of the rebellious object, an intimation of the absolute is affirmed.

In fact, this dramatization of the light's alternating appearance and disappearance, by its power to challenge and unseat the objectivized image, recharges and embodies the subjectivity of perception and interpretation. It explodes the objectivizing, deadening framework of vision; it revives the narrator's desire to see in nature signs of transcendence. This spot of light which suddenly seems to address him as if he were an exile resuscitates the challenging pursuit that makes sense of life, and launches him in quest of his hidden desire. This is the return of the subjective, or, as some would say, of the repressed–in any case, of the un-thought in a landscape. It is also the revenge, albeit imperfect and temporary, of the awareness of being-in-the-world upon the tyranny of the visible.

2. Illegibility of the Sign

This fault in the landscape where the presence is lodged is also a hermeneutic fault–exposing the uncertainness, the indeterminacy of things, that is to say the illegibility of signs. Melville thus ascribes to the shaft of light an essential irony–it is a clarity which is opaque to interpretation. This in turn enlarges the ironic scope of the veranda, whose claim to transparency is defeated by the rebellion of the sign, with its inherent opacity.

At first, the bit of light is only a sign, or more exactly an object which makes a sign–which beckons to man. It is reduced to a signifier, which can only be interpreted once the signified is reintegrated into it. Bewitched by this unstable apparition, whose intermittence is reminiscent of Moby Dick's breaches and plunges, the narrator is suddenly dispossessed of his mastery over things; his heart is eaten by worry and desire, just as "cankerous worms" gnaw at the blossoms in his pastoral paradise (6). He feels *called* to launch his quest for the meaning of this sign, like Moses summoned to ascend Sinai (5).

Finding fault with the initial naïveté of the narrator, the absolute (or more exactly, its possibility) returns to the foreground, out of the distance in which the picturesque esthetic sought to contain it. This uncertain object, by its unstable yet insistent being, captivates and intrigues the narrator, who, in a characteristic state of hyperacute self-consciousness, sees in it a sign *addressed to him*, glimpsed through an opening in a reality that is too smooth to be true, a sign apparently sanctified by the appearance of a rainbow (5), the traditional "token of the covenant," in Genesis, between God and his earthly creatures.

Joy in such a beauty could be enough for the solitary soul retired in the country, could be a sufficient sign of grace unto him. But no, he must have his misgivings about it. Like a modern doubting Thomas questioning Christ, he wants to make of this "uncertain object" an object of knowledge and not of faith. He must track it visually and bodily, must bring it back to reason, in other words, to a human proportion, avoiding the scandal of this fugitive word.

And so another border or threshold is drawn, the one which separates the world that can be sensed from a hypothetical beyond. The idea of the picturesque landscape could easily make sense of the first threshold, between the cultivated world and the wild world, by humanizing the space that it prolonged by means of the eye rather than the hand, but this new border presents greater difficulties. Is there any hope that a radically different perspective can order the relationship between the world we sense and the "backstage" world? Their long-established homothetic relationship was based in religion and represented by natural theology, which rested on a teleological and providentialist conception of the natural order[205] and its correlate, the typological interpretation of natural signs, perceived as "Images or Shadows of Divine Things."[206]

Melville is among the tormented heirs to this tradition, for whose practitioners the physical world appeared as the word of God, on a par with Holy Writ. He is among those who, historically and personally, questioned this relationship, which had begun to disintegrate or at least had become less certain. Melville's symbol of this uncertainty, as we have seen, is the intermittent light perceived in the mountains by the narrator in "The Piazza." While other Americans of the same period (notably Church) kept this threshold and this relationship intact—while still others (notably Emerson and Thoreau) forged ahead into immanentism—Melville, as incapable of believing as of not believing,[207] struggled incessantly with this anguishing question. As he wrote in *Pierre*:

---

[205] See especially William Paley, *Natural Theology; or, Evidences of the Existence and Attributes of the Deity, collected from the Appearances of Nature* (1825), a work famous in its day: "There cannot be a design without a designer; contrivance, without a contriver... Arrangement, disposition of parts, subserviency of means to an end, relation of instruments to a use, imply the presence of intelligence and mind" (Walls 20).

[206] The title of an important work by Jonathan Edwards (1703-1758), who interpreted the realities of the physical world as signs or "types" of spiritual realities.

[207] Cf. p. 149.

> Say what some poets will, Nature is not so much
> her own ever-sweet interpreter, as the mere
> supplier of that cunning alphabet, whereby
> selecting and combining as he pleases, each man
> reads his own peculiar lesson according to his
> own peculiar mind and mood.[208]

3. Signs and Substance

More specifically, it seems to me that "The Piazza" does not simply allude to Thoreau, but opposes him fundamentally, based on an entirely contrasting world view. Melville's challenge to Thoreau can be summarized as follows: how can one take this light for mere beauty–as substance and not a sign?

Thoreau–at least the most avowedly transcendental Thoreau, the one Melville would have read–seems to see in the world of nature the manifest presence of a divinity which requires only attention to attain meaning.[209] In Thoreau's world, brilliant signs are only waiting to be read. This is not a "blank" world carrying the stigma of being unwritten or illegible, but the immaculate glory of physical beauty:

> This plain sheet of snow which covers the ice of
> the pond, is not such a blancness [sic] as is
> unwritten, but such as is unread. All colors are in
> white. It is such simple diet to my senses as the
> grass and sky. There is nothing fantastic in them.
> Their simple beauty has sufficed men from the
> earliest times.–they have never criticised the
> blue sky and the green grass.[210]

---

[208] Melville 1971, 342.

[209] On the Thoreauvian theme of alertness, see for example the Journal, Feb. 8, 1857: "Music is perpetual, and only hearing is intermittent" (JIX:245).

[210] J1:207.

Thoreau makes himself the interpreter of presence, and not of signs. In Thoreau there is no separation between the object and the subject of perception–between *seer* and *seen*. In this form of transcendentalism, nature offers no message hidden behind its appearance, it is itself the divine. It is not a question of interpreting nature but, in a movement of fusion or communion with it, of participating in the divine. Resolutely situating his work on the side of sensory experience, of a being-in-the-world illuminated by interior light, Thoreau declares in his Journal:

> Beauty is where it is perceived. When I see the sun shining on the woods across the pond, I think this side the richer which sees it."[211]

Years later, Thoreau again evoked in his Journal the epiphany of a fleeting ray of light in these terms:

> It was but a transient ray, and there was no sunshine afterward, but the intensity of the light was surprising and impressive, like a halo, a glory in which only the just deserved to live. ... And then it was remarkable that the light-giver should have revealed to me, for all life, the heaving white breasts of those two ducks within this glade of light.[212]

In "The Piazza," conversely, God cannot be apprehended as *substance* inherent in things, but as a *sign* or *figure* in a universe of representation(s)–pictorial or theatrical. Divinity is no longer the organizer and the guarantor of a functioning natural theology which reads a shaft of light as a manifest sign of

---

[211] J1:205.

[212] JX:133-34; Oct. 28, 1857. Space prevents citing and discussing the entire passage.

the divine,[213] but a simple indecipherable trace, revealing a crisis of meaning. Melville's God is not a hidden God, but a God who plays hide and seek, and in this on-and-off fluttering, this intermittance of the absolute, the quest to be saved, to be chosen of God, takes place.

We might say that Melville's writing, at its greatest, makes us think and seek, whereas Thoreau's, adhering to a world of the senses that is the entire dwelling of the divine, becomes a source of contemplation and meditation, and an agent of transformation. Thoreau the reformer, Melville the interrogator: here we have the traditional critical contrast between Thoreau's (Emerson-derived) "optimism" and Melville's skepticism. Precisely, the narrator of "The Piazza" refuses contemplation in favor of questioning: Melville cannot or will not apprehend the world in the manner of Thoreau. Hence, "The Piazza" can be read as a metaphor for the errancy that is the destiny of those who insist on doubting.

In Melville's tale we behold the Calvinist drama of God's elect and God's grace. This writing is theatre: the narrative dramatizes the adventure of the subject, the questioner. Significantly, "The Piazza" makes constant reference to the theatre and to the scenic universe of perspective.

III. The Quest

For now we see through a glass, darkly; but
then face to face: now I know in part; but then I
shall know even as also I am known.
–I Cor. 13:12

The entirety of "The Piazza" appears as a commentary–negative–on this affirmation of the apostle Paul, which is commonly interpreted to mean that the indirect and confused knowledge of God that is mirrored obscurely by creation will be

---

[213] God literally *is* light in Christian scripture (John 1:5).

replaced by direct, clear, face-to-face experience of Deity in eternal life. Until now, the narrator on his veranda has seen only through a glass, darkly (5). The third act of the story tells of his quest for meaning, his search for that direct knowledge on the mountainside where the ray of light appears. Crossing beyond the "plane" of the "painting"–or stepping into the mirror–the narrator journeys toward what he imagines as a wonderland, in hope of a face-to-face encounter with "the fairy queen" (6).

Abandoning the rather facetious humor of the first part of the tale, the narrator is now confined to the elucidation of a mystery, the comprehension of which he associates directly with madness. Defeated by the esthetic world view, he succumbs to a metaphysical vertigo in a parable that, on the esthetic level, seems a revenge of the *capriccio* over the *veduta*.[214] If the first act of "The Piazza" echoed *Walden*, the narrative of the quest corresponds to a passage from *A Week on the Concord and Merrimack Rivers*, another work by Thoreau that Melville knew first hand.[215] The passage, a digression in the second chapter, recounts an excursion by Thoreau in 1844 to the same Mount Greylock that is visible from Melville's piazza.[216] Thoreau's passage is an archetype of the transcendentalist epiphany, affirming the spiritual dimension of light perceived in a moment of revelation. Beginning his ascent, Thoreau portrays himself as a pilgrim in the expectation of a revelation:

> It seemed a road for the pilgrim to enter upon
> who would climb to the gates of heaven. Now I

---

[214] In the original sense, *capriccio* designated a particularly inventive treatment of the design of architecture represented in a picturesque context. More generally, it has also served to characterize a pre-Romantic recourse to the powers of the imagination, as is shown, for example, by Tiepolo's *Capricci* or, even more famous, *Los Caprichos* of Goya.

[215] We know that Melville borrowed a copy from his friend Duyckinck in 1850. (Borst, 167)

[216] Thoreau calls Greylock by its former name, Saddleback, in *A Week*.

> crossed a hay-field, and now over the brook on a
> slight bridge, still gradually ascending all the
> while with a sort of awe, and filled with
> indefinite expectations as to what kind of
> inhabitants and what kind of nature I should
> come to at last.[217]

These dreamed inhabitants could be none other than demigods,
Thoreau suggests:

> It seemed as if he must be the most singular and
> heavenly minded man whose dwelling stood
> highest up the valley. (182)

Having arrived at the top of the mountains, Thoreau can
celebrate the sublimity of his vision and the new dimension of
his existence:

> As the light in the east steadily increased, it
> revealed to me more clearly the new world into
> which I had risen in the night, the new *terra
> firma* perchance of my future life. ...
> It was a favor for which to be forever silent to
> be shown this vision. The earth beneath had
> become such a flitting thing of lights and
> shadows as the clouds had been before. It was
> not merely veiled to me, but it had passed away
> like the phantom of a shadow, ...and this new
> platform was gained. As I had climbed above
> storm and cloud, so by successive days'
> journeys I might reach the region of eternal day,
> beyond the tapering shadow of the earth...
> (188-89)

---

[217] Thoreau 1980b, 181.

Similarly to Thoreau's depiction of his surroundings in *A Week*, the narrator of "The Piazza" mythologizes the countryside, yet takes it to an extreme, as if to caricature Thoreau's style before discounting his philosophy in the rest of the story. Such ironic presentation is more evidence that Melville's narrator functions as a parodist and critic of transcendentalism.

Outside this visual paradise, which has actually been a prison or tomb,[218] the questioner of signs undertakes his search for meaning. It would seem, though, beyond its humorous style and plenitude of literary allusions, that his vision is a mere hallucination, the product of too much reading, a metaphysical dissatisfaction serenely belied by everyday factuality. Taking Edmund Spenser as his guide, who turns out to be a far cry from Dante's Virgil (6), the narrator "launches his yawl" (his horse, actually) on a voyage that evokes the symbolic pilgrim's progress of life, or of the soul toward eternal life, as illustrated notably by Thomas Cole.[219] Borrowing the convention of the moralized landscape, the narrator of "The Piazza" undertakes his voyage surrounded by a retinue of guides and guardian angels who serve as witnesses of his revived faith (6, 7). As he navigates toward the mountain (the first of the enchanted islands of the *Piazza Tales*), he comes across animals whose somnambulous lethargy prefigures that of the only human inhabitants.

The approach to the cottage takes him through a "craggy pass" that slips through "a rent ... in [the] ragged sides" of nearby cliffs (7), before opening onto the dwelling, which is set among "fantastic rocks" (8). (The archetype of the "naturalized" house was idealized and popularized in the picturesque "villa

---

[218] Having compared his piazza to a "bench" in a painting gallery (2), the narrator later makes the explicit connection "The bench, the bed, the grave" (9).

[219] *The Voyage of Life*, series of four paintings (1842), National Gallery of Art, Washington, DC.

books"[220] of the day.) To the narrator his cottage at first appears the symbol of a perfect continuity between art and nature ("Nature, and but nature, house and all" 8), just as Thoreau often envisioned.[221] Accordingly, Marianna's cottage appears as the mirror image of the narrator's veranda, supposedly his source of an unbroken relationship with nature. However, this is a false symmetry: for the veranda commanded a countryside smooth and unragged, whereas the cottage is rather buried in the roughness of wild nature. The side of the cottage exposed to the north is totally opaque, "doorless and windowless" (8).

At the end of the narrator's quest, then, the ray of light turns out to be no more than a reflection on the sloping roof of the rundown house. Endowed with two faces, one brilliant, the other dark, this house embodies ambiguity in the same way as the tortoise of "The Encantadas."[222] The clearing itself is actually only a chiaroscuro, a new painting after the fashion of depicting ruined cottages in a stormy natural setting. Since this part of the tale only reaffirms the picturesque instead of providing the sublime revelation we expected, it expresses the failure of the quest. The light proves to be epiphanic, a simple, ambiguous sign that in no way suggests the radiance of another world. There is no unleashing of the sublime, no bolt of lightning that would explain and justify the light. The ascent of the mountain does not give rise to any ecstatic surge of knowledge or faith, or to any presence of God such as experienced by Moses "whom the Lord knew face to face" on Sinai or Pisgah.[223]

And now we have the narrator, like a disenchanted Moses, sitting on a stool in silence, realizing the emptiness of this ironical fairyland, where there is nothing magic left except

---

[220] See Maynard, 303-25. Let us note Melville's touch of humor when he states that the clapboards are "innocent of paint" (8); the satirical vocabulary echoes the demonization of all human ornamentation.

[221] See in particular Thoreau's description of the pioneers' houses in *The Maine Woods*.

[222] See Chapter 9.

[223] Deut. 34:10. On "Pisgah sight," cf. Landow 1980, 205-31.

the dismal sonority of the word *fairy* itself, repeated three times like a distant echo of the Trinity.[224]

This ironic fairy queen can offer no moral revelation to the narrator, and the desired face-to-face encounter, though it haunts the words they exchange (11), arrives at no instant of grace. Whereas Thoreau, on Mount Greylock, imagined he was ascending by degrees toward absolute revelation, Marianna, in contrast, is borne downward. She arrived in this dwelling not by progress in self-discovery through a new relationship with nature, but by a long descent toward nothingness. This orphan seems to be the sole survivor from a far side that is henceforth empty; it is as if she could say, like that other orphan whose cry resounds in the extreme circumstances of *Moby-Dick*: "And I only an escaped alone to tell thee."[225] She came to settle on the mountainside, yet still dreams of going further down, setting her gaze and her dreams on the sparkling of the narrator's house in the plain. She does not suppose it is a sign addressed to her, but simply imagines it as the place of earthly happiness, the symmetrical opposite of her dilapidated house, without giving it the slightest extra meaning.

Just as the narrator fancied he would set his gaze on "some happy mountain girl" (6), so Marianna imagines going down to the plain to "look upon whoever the happy being is that lives there" (12). Marianna, like the narrator, is one of those who has to see and touch in order to believe. "Blessed are those who have not seen and yet have believed"–Christ's words to doubting Thomas, which make salvation the fruit of faith rather than knowledge, are brought to mind by "The Piazza." They seem to shed light on the story's theme of seeing and its emphasis on

---

[224] Likewise, we seem to hear a far-off trinitarian echo in the triple repetitions of empty words in: "Near by–ferns, ferns, ferns; further–woods, woods, woods; beyond–mountains, mountains, mountains; then–sky, sky, sky" (9).

[225] Job 1:19, used as the epigraph of *Moby Dick*, at the end of which Ishmael escapes the shipwreck, Christ-like, in a coffin, and lives to tell the tale.

man's inability to move from the visible toward the invisible, to transcend sensory data, so long as he enjoys a world of the senses which can never be the world of sense ("feast[s] upon the view," 2).

Far from evoking the transcendent realm of eternal life, Marianna's clearing is an ambiguous place, not so much a threshold as "a pass between two worlds, participant of neither" (8). And Marianna is not the image of some promise of salvation: she incarnates neither faith nor hope, but seems to bear on her shoulders the weight of an obscure guilt. Pale, solitary and tired–"a lonely girl," "a pale-cheeked girl" (8) with a "weary face" (12)–she reminds us of that other Melville character, Bartleby. They are both more figures than characters–figures of an uninhabitable in-between, living dead, or more exactly, as Dieter Meindl describes them, beings who are "living their death."[226] Having come from the other side of a mountain which forms the border between two worlds, a mountain of which she is (with her brother who is even more a ghost) the only inhabitant, the solitary Marianna, whose retirement has nothing peaceful about it, seems to be nothing less than an orphan of God, condemned to remain in a sort of purgatory between life and death, getting on with her sewing like Bartleby with his copying. Isn't she also, like Bartleby, one of those otherworldly creatures who "lives without dining" (45)?

IV. Theatre and Illusion

The ascent of the mountain is a symbol not so much of asceticism as of the errancy of Thoreau's "men of little faith [who] stand only by their feet–or recline on the ground, having lost their reliance on the soul,"[227] an image of wandering astray or of death.

---

[226] Meindl 100.
[227] Journal, J1:204.

Undertaken from nostalgia for a "book of nature" which would be only a prophecy, the narrator's quest appears as a vain attempt to become one with his vision. On the mountain there is produced no revelation, no epiphany or appearance of God, but only a face-to-face encounter with the absent Face. Everything in this episode speaks of absence and withdrawal of all meaning, the dissociation of the human (brother/sister; Marianna/narrator), that of the human from nature, and that of nature itself–as is suggested by the two hop-vines on poles which "would have ...joined over in an upward clasp, but... trailed back whence they sprung" (12). Between the narrator and Marianna there is neither a face-to-face encounter nor recognition, only an encounter in a play of mirrors. If the purpose of the quest was to reintegrate the signified into the signifier that seemed dissociated from it–like the matching halves of the *sumbolon* ("symbol"), the token used in mystic ritual–then the lack of recognition between the narrator and Marianna shows the irremediable dissociation of the two halves–that is, the impossibility of making a symbol out of the sign. This failure once more plunges the narrator into the abyss which separates the esthetic from the religious. In other words, light as a sign cannot really signify, but only designate this abyss.

By building his veranda, the narrator proclaims his desire to become one with his vision, but he turns out to be the prisoner of a world governed by a principle of dissociation that is poorly masked by the sentimental and vain order of the picturesque. And the veranda turns out to be merely an ironic avatar of Plato's cave. Formulated in strictly Platonic terms, "The Piazza" reaches resolution in the recognition and affirmation of the fallacious character of light–the luminous can no longer claim to be the "numinous"–which amounts to a disavowal of Platonic idealism. Condemned to watching the shadows filing past on the shimmering wall of the amphitheatre of mountains which rises before him, the narrator, at the end of his quest, must give up all hope of attaining that union of the Beautiful and the True which Plato held to be the supreme Good.

The result of the quest is not an uplifting mystical interpretation or a revelation of divinity, but the disillusioned discovery that behind the appearances, there is nothing. Powerless to transcend by his gaze this world of impotent signs, and thus deprived of the real meaning of appearance, the narrator succumbs to the vertigo of a radical illusion of the world as merely a devil's farce–just an episode in the "old wars of Lucifer and Michael" (5).[228]

From this mountaintop that he had imagined as proof of the absolute, the narrator now departs, proclaiming an ignorance–"I, too, know nothing…" (12)–which seems to enable an entirely worldly wisdom, for the time being. Having renounced the absolute along with any other "backstage" essences, resigned to the reign of illusion, he delights in the spectacle of a picturesque nature where landscape and stage-set are but one–"Yes, the scenery is magical–the illusion so complete" (12). As if it were Plato's cave itself, and not a transcendent kingdom, which is the true home of humanity. Expressing his skepticism with regard to any religious or visionary experience, Melville's story flatly rejects all faith in the redemptive powers of art as of nature. In this regard, "The Piazza" is a cautionary tale.

With his desire of transcendence thwarted, the narrator concludes that it is not only the representation of the world which is theatre–as conceived by a stagecraft of the picturesque–but the world itself. Resigned to the world's theatricality in terms reminiscent of Jacques's "All the world's a stage,"[229] the narrator also seems kin to the post-transcendental Emerson of "Experience," who seems to deny all esthetic or metaphysical depth when he declares, "We live amid surfaces, and the true art of life is to skate well on them."[230] It is as if, in "The Piazza," the

---

[228] Jonathan Edwards suggested this possibility in "A Divine and Supernatural Light": "We cannot determine but that the devil, who transforms himself into an angel of light, may cause imaginations of an outward beauty, or visible glory" (*Norton* 395).

[229] Shakespeare, *As You Like It*, 2:7:139.

[230] Emerson 1983, 395.

Romantic quest for an absolute which will transcend immediate experience is contained within a baroque drama where the world appears a theatre. It is significant that Melville's story ends with imagery of that baroque genre *par excellence*, the opera ("My box-royal... my theatre of San Carlo... my prima donna," 12). The baroque is a complex concept, but if we may generalize at least that it traditionally involves theatricality–appearance and not essence, effect and not substance, the visual and not the intellectual–then Melville's world-view seems to partake of a baroque esthetics.

It is a vision of the world that hews to the borderline between sense and nonsense. Acutely aware of dwelling in a world of sight-lines and optical illusion, deprived of the transparency of the world and of meaning–and with all his projects reduced to impenetrable masks or surfaces–man thus becomes the victim of contemporary subjectivity, according to which the subject is the source of the real world.

Just when it seems we will be plunged into the joyful and hopeless recognition of a theatricality of human existence that borders upon the absurd, the end of the play brings us an unhoped-for truth. The lights go down, our vision is cloaked in darkness, the curtain falls. Now the real ghosts can begin their vertiginous reign–the shadows of an exacting truth. Freed of the mirages offered by that *camera lucida* of the grotesque, the veranda, the narrator will surrender to the world of the *camera obscura*, the dark chamber of his dreams and nightmares, persuaded that "truth comes in with darkness" and not with the simulations of stage-lighting. Directing our gaze toward the tales which are to follow "The Piazza," Melville foreshadows its fall along an axis of reality which is not the sunlit, comforting theatre of the picturesque but that, nocturnal and unsettling, of the grotesque.

9

Prophecy and the Grotesque in Melville's "Encantadas"

"Truth comes in with darkness," as we have seen in "The Piazza," but in what form? Once night has fallen, and with it the curtain over the stage–once the reason of the world offered by the picturesque perspective has faded away–the stage is set for the parade of monsters "bred by the sleep of reason," in Goya's famous phrase. Underlying the often-discussed unity of Melville's series of sketches titled "The Encantadas; or, Enchanted Isles," we may discern a half-imaginary stage on which the actors in a grotesque theatre, both animal and human, follow one another.

I. Narrator and persona

When "The Encantadas" was first published in 1854, the author declined his identity by means of an obvious pseudonym. Thus we are very carefully notified that we are not facing the author himself but a mask, a borrowed identity, the source of a complex narrative instance. A rare practice in Melville,[231] the pseudonym casts a particularly interesting light on the nature of this work.

Our fictitious author calls himself "Salvator R. Tarnmoor." This scarcely veiled reference to Salvator Rosa, the great seventeenth-century champion of picturesque painting,[232]

---

[231] He used it only in "Hawthorne and His Mosses."
[232] See the biography by Scott (1995).

provides a strong thematic continuity with "The Piazza." Further, it allows us to imagine that the narrative voice of "The Piazza" is that of an artist who has come to the countryside looking for a source of inspiration, and that this artist, having disavowed the sunny side of the picturesque and revealed dark nature as the basis of all true art, is none other than the author of this series of ten sketches, "The Encantadas." Melville explicitly suggests as much when his narrator describes himself as "far from the influences of towns and proportionally nigh to the mysterious ones of nature" and recalling his experience of the islands "as in a dream" (129).[233]

The conceit of a literary work composed by a painter was certainly not new, and in the context of nineteenth-century American literature the use of the word *sketch* necessarily recalls the famous *Sketch-Book* of Washington Irving, published in 1819. By presenting it as the work of a certain "Geoffrey Crayon, Gent.," Irving suggested an analogy between his writerly art and that of the painter. It is important, however, to note that the pseudonym chosen by Melville does not simply reflect artistic practice in general, but refers to a particular artist.

I would suggest, indeed, that we will understand this series of sketches better once we realize that it is fictitiously the work of an artist-narrator, more precisely a painter whose rebellious and sulphurous reputation fascinated the Romantics. Even in his own time, Salvator Rosa had intrigued the public. His carefully self-cultivated image seemed to symbolize the independence, at once fantastical and melancholic, of genius. The Romantic era cloaked Rosa in the dark aura of the rebel, like an early Lord Byron–the painter of bandits and sorcerers in dark passageways and tortuous landscapes thus appeared as the apostle of rebellion, a righter of society's wrongs, the spokesman of outlaws who opposed tyranny.[234]

---

[233] Page references in parentheses are to Melville 1987.

[234] Rosa's romantic image owes much to his first biography by Lady Sidney Morgan, *The Life and Times of Salvator Rosa* (1824).

Melville's narrator thus appears as an avatar of Rosa when he introduces himself as a "lover of the picturesque" and offers us one of his own compositions featuring "some tatterdemallion outlaw" emerging from the "dark cavernous recesses" of the Encantadas' harsh landscape (138). It is especially important to keep this relationship in mind in instances such as Sketch VI, in which the narrator, as though fascinated by the magic of evil, adopts a murky rhetoric which tends to attenuate the savagery of the "Buccaneers."[235] And in case we are tempted to think that he is only using words he does not subscribe to, we have only to look back at Sketch IV with its mention of "loyal freebooters" and an "excellent Buccaneer" (141-42) to see the favorable bias in his point of view. Listening to this great rebel of a narrator, we often hear something like the demon's snicker. Doesn't he go as far as justifying the behavior of the Dog-King, undertaking to convince us of the well-foundedness of the unjustifiable (164-65)? Unless, precisely, this is meant to provoke us, making us react to a tone resembling the satirical voice of Jonathan Swift.[236] Indeed Melville's whole series of sketches presents this ambiguous tone, this moral chiaroscuro, where the most monstrous creatures seem presented in a relatively benevolent manner. What dominates is the figure of the narrator who lacks neutrality, not just because he inevitably has a point of view but because he seems to have taken sides.

II. A Universe of Disorientation

1. Failure of Sight

More precisely than "descriptive tales" in the manner of Irving or Hawthorne, Melville's episodes are intended as a painter's sketches; in fact they are intensely visual. They are all

---

[235] For example, Sketch VI, 145-46.
[236] Especially that masterpiece of irony, *A Modest Proposal* (1729).

the more stimulating to the imagination in the context of Melville's mistrust of systems: a sketch is less formal, more immediate, than a rigid easel painting.

In the first sketch then, the narrator proposes to outline for us "the general aspect of the Encantadas" (126). Endowed with a pencil stroke as swift as it is evocative, the artist from the outset eliminates the conventions of the picturesque (a vision of an order whose harmony is heightened by a few touches of irregularity) in order to set us in the heart of a universe that is resolutely somber and hostile to man. It is the mirror reversal of the pastoral paradise dear to a whole tradition of painting. This world will be just as infernal as the one evoked at the beginning of "The Piazza" was paradisal, as if the narrator were answering his own admonition that he must not neglect the "dark side" of the symbolic tortoise (Sketch II, 130).

These opposite sides find their pictorial counterpart in the classical contrast between Claude Lorrain and Salvator Rosa.[237] The former was famed for his landscapes of an ideal perfection inspired by antiquity but actually situated outside time. Inversely, the darker, rougher, wilder pictures of Rosa gave more importance to the destructive power of time. This dichotomy is reflected in the two settings of Melville's theatre— the ideal pastoral landscape of "The Piazza" and the infernal one of "The Encantadas." Just as "The Piazza" begins by presenting an orderly and well-organized vision of the world, the guarantee of its comforting closeness, everything in "The Encantadas" defamiliarizes our relationship to the world and sparks an uncomfortable feeling of alienation. What the painter-narrator shows us is a landscape in negative, whose obsessive presence— like that of Bartleby—is actually defined by its deficiency "in what landscape painters call 'life,'" to borrow Melville's expression in "Bartleby the Scrivener" (14). As we have seen "The Piazza," Melville will have nothing to do with a life which is not one, but only a grotesque simulacrum which *apes* life.

---

[237] See notably Scott 227-28, as well as Manwaring.

Even if he ultimately agrees that everything is only illusion, he is referring to nothing less than the existential illusion itself–profound, significant and troubling.

The narrator's gallery of landscapes evokes not so much the Galápagos as the Phlegrean Fields near Naples, a required stop on any European tour.[238] He introduces the Encantadas abruptly, with a narrative so disjointed that it could almost be the product of the same plague of fires that produced the islands themselves:

> Take five-and-twenty heaps of cinders dumped
> here and there in an outside city lot... A group ...
> looking much as the world at large might, after a
> penal conflagration. (126)

This image of an anti-world is scandalous in many respects, not least because it conjures up a modern cityscape and so ruins forever any chance of association with a pastoral paradise. It finds a stunning echo in a famous journal passage in which Nathaniel Hawthorne tells of encountering Melville around Liverpool,

> wandering to and fro over these deserts, as
> dismal and monotonous as the sandhills amidst
> which we were sitting. He can neither believe,
> nor be comfortable in his unbelief.[239]

Certainly these landscapes, like the dreams and nightmares evoked later (132), are an expression of that truth born of darkness foreshadowed in the closing lines of "The Piazza." Such a mental landscape in the tradition of the *capriccio* after Piranesi has nothing to do with the picturesque scenes known as *vedute*, which significantly were often *isolari*, or

---

[238] Melville would visit the place himself in 1856. See his *Journal of a Visit to Europe and the Levant* (Melville 1955), and cf. Chapter 10.

[239] Nov. 12, 1856 (Leyda 2:529).

views of the thirty-odd islands in the Venetian Lagoon.[240] And if the spirit of the place is resident here, it is not the *genius loci* dear to the picturesque painters, but a spirit which moans like Dante's damned: "'Have mercy upon me,' the wailing spirit of the Encantadas seems to cry..." (126).

Disavowing the picturesque esthetic as well as topographical literature, Melville's sketches constantly emphasize the illusion of a sovereignty of vision, of an entire visibility and intelligibility of the landscape. This glassy world would perhaps remind us of the "wilderness of glass" in Edgar Allan Poe's "City of the Sea" (1845), except that it does not suggest transparency in any way (the vitrified lava of the Encantadas is opaque); it conveys rather the murky immobility of Bartleby's universe.

This negative landscape then, this hollow world seemingly emptied of substance, is defined only by what it lacks. To these volcanic rocks deprived of the life dear to the landscapist, "change never comes" and "rain never falls." These lands are uninhabited, not frequented even by "the outcasts of the beasts," the jackals.[241] Symbolizing the sterility of the land, the shrubs are thorny, "without fruit and without a name." As for the soundscape, it too is vacant, reduced to the degree zero of sound articulation: "No voice, no low, no howl is heard; the chief sound of life here is a hiss."

The narrator describes a landscape haunted by biblical resonances; the imagery of annihilation and desolation ("penal conflagration," "curse") evokes the language of the Hebrew prophets: "I will make waste mountains and hills, and dry up all their herbs; and I will make the rivers islands, and I will dry up

---

[240] The best known of these collections of views of the islands surrounding Venice is the *Ventiquattro prospettive di isole della Laguna de Venezia* drawn by Francesco Tironi and engraved by Antonio Sardi (1790).

[241] These and the following citations from "The Encantadas" are on 126-27.

the pools."[242] In his poem "Clarel: A Poem and Pilgrimage in the Holy Land," Melville explicitly compares the landscapes of the Galápagos and those of Palestine.[243]

The landscapes are so dark that Melville's pseudonymous reference to Rosa appears half-ironic, joined as it is to a second name which submerges it. Tarnmoor, by its double suggestion of a *tarn* (mountain lake or pool) and a *moor*, underlines the disparity between Rosa's landscapes and those of "The Encantadas," which are almost entirely arid.[244]

Melville's pen-name introduces another theme of "The Encantadas." Indeed, if *moor* designates a kind of terrain, its homonym also denotes anchorage. Precisely, however, all suggestion of stability–of picturesque scenery and the gaze we cast upon it–is totally demolished at the very outset. (As opposed to Thoreau, Melville would certainly not dream of a *terra firma*.[245]) The title of Melville's first sketch, "The Isles at Large," with its play on the meanings of "in general" and "at liberty," is an ironic commentary on the validity of an encyclopedic discourse that concerns a fundamentally unstable and unknowable world. Throughout these sketches, the narrator keeps emphasizing the fallible and even unadapted character of perception, whose grotesque symbol is the tortoise which cannot recognize and surmount obstacles:

> I found him butted like a battering-ram against
> the immovable foot of the foremast, and still

---

[242] Isaiah 42:15. Chapters 41-43 of Isaiah form a subtext that is essential to the reading of "The Encantadas."

[243] *Clarel*, published in 1876, was based on Melville's tour. Cf. also Chapter 10.

[244] True, Rosa resisted the search for the ideal landscape and favored a more convulsive beauty often called picturesque, though in Rosa it is not remotely concerned with balance or harmony. Still, this master of the dark picturesque appears too confident, too radiant, to satisfy Melville, whose chosen pen-name is clearly ironic.

[245] Cf. p. 137.

striving, tooth and nail, to force the impossible
passage. (132)

Nowhere is this critique more manifest than in Sketch
IV. In this farcical piece the narrator plays the moralist, waxing
ironical about all conventions and certainties, and laughing at
human vanities. He begins thus by deflating any heroic
pretension–the explorers' or tourists', no matter–and he breezily
avoids the problem of how to climb the rock, bearing us upward
as though by magic (137).

Melville's view from aloft–a staging and dramatization
of a gaze whose impotence is evident everywhere we try to
look–undermines the traditional heroism of gazing upon the sea
from on high, as we have known it in narratives of exploration
beginning with Xenophon's soldiers beholding the Black Sea
from Mount Theches and continuing through Keats's Cortez and
his men gazing upon the Pacific, "silent upon a peak in Darien."

> Look edgeways... You see nothing; but permit
> me to point out the direction, if not the place, of
> certain interesting objects in the vast sea, which
> kissing this tower's base, we behold unscrolling
> itself towards the Antarctic Pole. (137)

So the smooth-talking artist seeks to subjugate the
reader: the unscrupulous braggart makes fun of those whom he
claims to be enlightening, inviting us to take his droll travelogue
for the real thing. Borrowing his language from the tourist
guides, he describes for us an expanse of nothingness with an
almost credible verve and drive. He strives to bring this vacant
landscape to life like a native guide rhapsodizing over a meagre
heap of ruins. Employing amusing physical and verbal gestures
to conjure a vision of things that slip out of sight, using a wealth
of words as spellbinding and sonorous as an otherworldly
incantation, Melville's narrator is like a magician-guide who
mesmerizes his client while depleting his purse. This play

between the visible and the hidden, and the impossibility of framing nature, give rise to an ironical commentary on the picturesque as an object of touristic consumption, and indeed on the very possibility of representation. Dissolving the metaphysical notions of invisibility and infinity into that of the natural limits of perception, the narrator pitilessly discredits them both.

Once we sense it, Melville's irony appears everywhere. Thus for example the narrator refers us to far off, invisible landmarks yet speaks as if he has helped us gain an exact idea of our positioning in the midst of these extensive seascapes (139). Then, he directs our gaze again toward the desolate expanse of the Encantadas, an ironical version of Moses's view of the Promised Land from Pisgah as told in Deuteronomy 34. However, though the focus is nearer, he is still simply showing us the emptiness with ludicrous irony: "Where we still stand, here on Rodondo, we cannot see all the other isles, but it is a good place from which to point where they lie" (141).

In the same way that he discredits sight's pretension to sovereignty, the narrator deflates the seriousness of his descriptions, as in this image to help us visualize something inherently invisible, namely the equator:

> Well, that identical crater-shaped headland there,
> all yellow lava, is cut by the Equator exactly as a
> knife cuts straight through the centre of a pumpkin
> pie. (139)

Melville thus provides a grotesque image of the line that divides the two polarities of the real, and does so with a wink to the reader—pumpkins being traditionally associated with magicians.

With his running parody of the encyclopedic discourse and of expert tour guides, the narrator furnishes many details on the history of the islands, thus providing a "tour" of the Encantadas by the circularity of his ironically panoramic gaze as

much as by the completeness of a historical discourse in which
he pulls together all the legends, tales and anecdotes he can find
about the place (138-39). Painstaking in his effort at credibility,
he goes so far as to provide us with his bibliography, indicating
his sources with an earnest and winning concern for lucidity. Bit
by bit, indeed, we get the shady picture of a narrator/painter/sail-
or/tortoise-hunter/fisherman/naturalist/pirate/guide and man of
learning, in a waltz of identities that makes this magician a
trickster, a confidence man who puts on an act to beguile his
listeners, a real wordsmith and prince of appearances. Thus he
suggests to anyone who will listen that pirate and poet are one
and the same (142).

Each supposedly historical episode seems to warn that
appearances are deceiving, like so many parables of incertitude,
so that finally we wonder whether they are not all fabrications
intended to display his powers. This enchanter has rendered the
islands invisible or turned them into grotesque parodies of the
Fortunate Isles. He might be another Prospero; doesn't Oberlus
in Sketch IX claim to be born of Sycorax, the mother of Caliban
in *The Tempest*, borrowing Shakespeare's own dialogue at that
(164)? Just as Prospero manipulates events in Shakespeare's
play, it would seem that the narrator of "The Encantadas" is the
real director of each of its episodes.

2. Mirages of Knowledge

Manifestly, it is Salvator Rosa who is addressing us as a
character in Sketch III when the narrator evokes a picturesque
landscape in the tradition of the Neapolitan master (134), then
some "bandit birds" (135), and when he marvels as an artist in
the face of the colorful richness of living things. At first,
however, he leads us to imagine a much more murky universe,
that of a gray dawn whose atmosphere reminds us of "Benito
Cereno." This Rock Rodondo which, the narrator often reminds
us, is often mistaken from afar for the white sail of a ship (134,

137), is no less disturbing close up as our gaze sweeps across the spectrum of living creatures from the lowest to the highest–all of them contributing to the general cacophony, in a vision at once comic and terrifying. Here in fact is another aspect of the work of Rosa echoed in the world of "The Encantadas"–the grotesque creatures of the witchcraft scenes he painted in the 1640s. Watching for truth in the shadows, the narrator plunges his gaze into infernal regions void of light, where the choir of angels becomes a "demoniac din" (134), and where the order of the world is reduced to grotesque classifications of natural history– of which the ambiguous symbol is the penguin, "pertaining neither to Carnival nor Lent" (135). If the Encantadas confront us with a universe of disorientation and of the defeat of sight, they also underscore the failure of reason. The inadequacy of the categories by which man claims to understand the world only worsens the vertigo of perception.

This description is a surreal parody of scientific-naturalistic discourse, emphasizing the impossibility of a rational knowledge of that which is fleeting by nature. Melville's series of sketches of the Encantadas parodies the encyclopedic approach, the forms of knowing, the better to emphasize the impossibility of knowing and thus to acknowledge the ultimate reign of the formless. Given the unintelligibility of man and nature, any idea of scientific transactions appears as vain and corruptible as that of economic transactions. This work is constructed like a sum: a *summa* in the sense of an encyclopedic totality, a work seen as the sum of its parts, which surveys and tabulates all the narratives and bits of knowledge about these islands, but incorporates them badly if at all, creating a deformity, an asymmetry characteristic of the grotesque. The narrator employs the rules of encyclopedic style in order to mock them: this world in trompe-l'oeil shall have an encyclopedia in trompe-l'oeil.

Science appears incapable of describing a world which is hybrid by nature: it is not disposed to ambiguity and must even avoid it; there is no way for it to see the "two sides to a tortoise"

(130). This whole gallery of deformed and grotesque creatures (135) underlines the pointlessness of a science that presupposes the correspondence of its categories to reality, for boundaries in this world remain uncertain. The equator (139) fascinates us because this line of demarcation between one half of the world and the other is physically unlocatable; in the same way, natural creatures disconcert us by their non-compliance with distinctions of species or even of genus. The grotesque metaphor of the classification of the animal kingdom suggested by Rock Rodondo–attacking the central tenet of natural theology, the existence of an immanent order in the world–only prepares the way for the much more serious and problematic question of the definition of humanity in Sketches VII and IX. In other words, this scrutiny of the physical world symbolizes that of the metaphysical. In his study (1981), Wolfgang Kayser sees the grotesque as the mode expressing man's incapacity to orient himself in a universe that is fundamentally destabilizing,[246] which reveals him as a foreigner whose concepts and categories are just so many ludicrous, unworkable tools in his efforts to control the world. The grotesque always appears when a being (like the unclassifiable Bartleby) or a situation escapes from any frame, any control, creating an ambiguous mix of the frightful and the marvelous.

Every creature seems an orphan of God in this world of "The Encantadas"–a universe of dereliction from which God has disappeared, perhaps forever. God's withdrawal puts the intelligibility of the world at risk. How can man make sense of a world without God? Darwin basically postulates that the world has a meaning, although a very different one from that of natural theology.[247] In Darwin's world, there are no monsters. Although

---

[246] Kayser 185.

[247] H. Bruce Franklin and Agnès Derail have analyzed "The Encantadas" in relation to Darwin, who described his excursion to the Galápagos in *The Voyage of the Beagle* (1839). Although *The Origin of Species* (1859) appeared five years after "The Encantadas," Darwin's ideas about natural history had been clear enough in his prior publications.

this new world is resolutely non-anthropocentric (man is no longer the center of the Darwinian universe, but one element among others of an animal kingdom marked by processes of differentiation) and virtually God-less, the Darwinian revolution does not discount the intelligible, but seeks to restore it as based on a new understanding of nature. In "The Encantadas," if God has disappeared as a point of anchorage and reference, nature has not replaced him. Neither God, nor nature: Melville's universe is decidedly that of the in-between, just as if Melville resided in the empty space created by a wavering of meaning. The great and fundamental difference between these two authors' worlds is that Melville has not yet closed the book on the idea of the centrality of the divine, while Darwin undertakes to reestablish meaning in the world on a new basis. With Melville, everything continues to point toward a missing but still hoped-for God. Differently from Darwin, Melville's description of the Encantadas, even as a parody, is carried out in an anthropocentric mode which is also theocentric. Not that God's grandeur is manifest in the world; rather, his withdrawal from it is proclaimed. God's negative presence still amounts to a centrality.

Whereas "The Piazza" starts by postulating familiarity with the world, "The Encantadas" on the contrary brings about a fearsome experience of defamiliarization. Having *sketched* his stage with the minimalist, vaguely supernatural scenery of modern stagecraft, the painter-narrator of "The Encantadas" plays with conventions (encyclopedic, typological, scientific...) and offers us a phantasmagoria which is the nocturnal, theatrical truth of the world foreseen at the conclusion of "The Piazza." The lead actor in this theatre of shadows, the narrator-guide, embarks on his oneiric / ironic excursion at the heart of the archipelago, not unlike the procession of grotesque creatures–tortoises, penguins–that passes in front of us, disorienting our gaze and our expectations. This procession precedes the arrival of the "human" characters, prepares that mix of the comic and the frightful which transforms this monster rally into a metaphysical Barnum and Bailey.[248] As an ironical commentary on the vacuity of the picturesque sketch, Melville's "sketches" are really more like *skits*: the narrator-as-spectator, still settled in his box, but henceforth plunged into the darkness of dream and nightmare, sees nature unfolding not as the theatre of God, but as the theatre of the grotesque.

III. A Grotesque Theatre

Like a good number of esthetic categories, the idea of the grotesque has had a long history which has not clarified its meaning at all. Nevertheless it does have a number of formal characteristics generally acknowledged by scholars, and on this basis I shall risk applying it here to "The Encantadas."[249]

According to Kayser, the grotesque has had a double resonance since its first use in the Renaissance:

> By the word *grottesco* the Renaissance, which used it to designate a specific ornamental style suggested by antiquity, understood not only something playfully gay and carelessly fantastic, but also something ominous and sinister in the face of a world totally different from the familiar one–a world in which the realm of inanimate things is no longer separated from those of plants, animals, and human beings, and where the laws of statics, symmetry, and proportion are no longer valid.[250]

---

[248] With my description of the narrator as showman and trickster in mind, it is interesting to recall that P. T. Barnum, Melville's exact contemporary, dubbed himself the Prince of Humbugs.

[249] See especially, for the modern period, Kayser, Clayborough, and Thomson. Cook and Meindl have also drawn upon the idea of the grotesque to illuminate Melville's work.

[250] Kayser 21.

The difficulty, then, stems above all from an inherent ambiguity:

> The grotesque occurs in the border regions
> between fantasy and reality, beauty and ugliness,
> the tragic and the comic, the human and the non-
> human, the living and the dead, the demonic and
> the ludicrous.[251]

Connotations of the grotesque, then, will depend on one's accentuation of one or the other of its essential components. Schematically, we may trace two overall conceptions of the grotesque. One, deriving from Mikhail Bakhtin, emphasizes its comic dimension, linking the grotesque to the carnival. The second conception, following Kayser, is more tormented, bordering on absurdism: "The grotesque is a play with the absurd."[252]

Whichever approach one chooses, the basis of the grotesque consists in the creation of an *internal tension* between the incompatible elements, ensuring that the comic does not turn to the tragic. This fusion and this tension distinguish the grotesque from both the burlesque and the tragic, as well as from the tragicomic, as Philip Thomson suggests in terms which apply perfectly to the universe of "The Encantadas":

> Tragicomedy points only to the fact that life is
> alternately tragic and comic; the world is now a
> vale of tears, now a circus. The grotesque ... has
> a harder message. It is that the vale of tears and
> the circus are one, that tragedy is in some ways

---

[251] Gysin 27.
[252] Kayser 187. Although Kayser shows that historically the grotesque mingles the ridiculous with the terrible, his analysis accentuates its fearsome and disturbing aspects.

160

comic and all comedy in some way tragic and pathetic.[253]

One finds in Melville a good number of traits characteristic of the grotesque: the deformation of beings and things, their resemblance to clowns or marionettes, the ambiguous mixture of contradictory elements, the incongruity of forms and situations, the combination of the ridiculous and the terrible, all producing in the reader a disturbing feeling of strangeness, of defamiliarization. The grotesque appears as the perfect mode of consciousness in which man can recognize his situation as a foreigner in the world, his alienation: it is significant that Melville's characters are all "out of sync"–with the world, with themselves or their period–symbolic castaways or orphans. Strangeness does not mean unreality: the grotesque is distinct from a related mode, the fantastic (and its gothic version). The fantastic supposes a suspension of natural laws (an example is Franz Kafka's *The Metamorphosis*), an eruption of the irrational into ordinary reality which produces a suspense between the strange and the marvelous: "The fantastic is the hesitation felt by a being who knows only natural laws, in the face of an apparently supernatural event."[254] This sense of a break in reality remains foreign to the very structure of "The Encantadas."

The grotesque universe of disorientation and desubstantiation is also that of dehumanization, in which the challenging and derision of everything human appear in certain essential forms–the monster, the phantom, the puppet–all of which empty humanity of its substance.

Monstrous beings, half-human, half-animal, have been an essential characteristic of the grotesque from the beginning. And so, on the stage of "The Encantadas," we meet the hybrids Oberlus, part human, part reptile, or the Creole "Dog King" who, more than a king of dogs, is a King Dog, reflecting and

---
[253] Thomson 63.
[254] Todorov 29.

concentrating the blackness of the animals that serve him. Physical deformity is the reflection of the savagery of the soul, the visual translation of the moral ugliness and perversity of a humanity out of touch with itself. These monsters are the shadowy representations of the malignancy residing in human nature and society, embodied on stage for us to recognize.

The phantom may not be as present in "The Encantadas" (even though one sketch dramatizes the tale of a ghost ship), but it is a major theme in Melville. Bartleby, for example, is a phantom in the sense that he is "living his death," just like Marianna in "The Piazza."[255]

Finally the puppet, as a grotesque being, combines mechanical behavior with the appearance of life; his mechanical articulation symbolizes the disjointed and disembodied character of human existence. As Kayser writes:

> The mechanical object is alienated by being brought to life, the human being by being deprived of it. Among the most persistent motifs of the grotesque we find human bodies reduced to puppets, marionettes, and automata, and their faces frozen into masks.[256]

Among these robot-like characters belonging to the grotesque, we find Bartleby and Marianna, who are puppets as well as phantoms. The worrisome Bartleby always answers mechanically and with an impassive face; Marianna is completely reduced to her role of industrious seamstress. The guide-narrator of "The Encantadas" also sometimes seems to gesticulate feverishly, like a marionette, in a world too big to be seen, too vague to be grasped. All the characters of "The Encantadas," as they struggle deliriously with their will to power, seem to be disjointed by the uncontrolled movements of

---

[255] See Chapter 8.
[256] Kayser 183.

history, or by a madness the spectacle of which, Kayser affirms, "is one of the fundamental experiences of the grotesque."[257]

The grotesque universe is often charged with a compelling theatricalism. Thus "Bartleby the Scrivener" can appear as a series of skits in which the narrator sketches each new interpretation or reaction. Each sketch of "The Encantadas," as suggested earlier, is a skit acted out upon the islands' desolate stage, with its unity of place and action, its moment of tension and its climactic scene (the drowning of Felipe and Truxill, the struggle between Oberlus and his captive, the battle of the colonists and the dogs), and its power drawn from the combination of the pathetic and the ridiculous, the tragic and the comic. Ultimately, what joins most of these characters together in spite of the fragmentation of place and literary structure are those hybrid creatures, the tortoises, whose grotesque gait sets the tone for the whole series of sketches. The Galápagos tortoise, endowed with a mythical and supernatural dimension crystallizing the archaic fears of humanity (129, 132), is a veritable idol in the biblical sense, that is to say the grotesque image *par excellence*. Worshippers of this idol–which symbolizes all the materialistic aspirations of man (food, hunting, market value) and beyond that, a whole economic and social system–all those who happen to pass through these islands lose their way and are brought down, conquered by this modern Mammon whose illustrious predecessor is the white whale, Moby Dick.

IV. Mirages of identity

"They shall be turned back, they shall be greatly ashamed, that trust in graven images, that say to the molten images, 'Ye are our gods.'"
–Isaiah 42:17

---

[257] Kayser 184.

Just as the first part of "The Encantadas" presented a world resistant to visual apprehension and conceptual definition, so the second part presents mirages of identity–a theme whose corollary is the question of sovereignty, whether it be over one's self or over a territory and a political body.

Each of the characters of "The Encantadas" appears as a grotesque incarnation of Emersonian self-reliance and self-renewal, breaking with the weight of the past and of individual history. Believing in the possibility of rebuilding their existence, they venture forth in an attempt to take their destiny in hand. At this point, one more connotation of the word "sketch" resounds, that of existence as a *sketch of being*, of the contours of a redesigned life, the individual being motivated by a belief in moral perfectionism, the corollary of the transcendentalist credo of the divinity of man–in fact, nothing other than a reformulation of the notion of moral perfectibility inherited from Enlightenment philosophy.

Quite the opposite, Melvillean skepticism sees in man the grotesque creature *par excellence*, half divine, half bestial. For at bottom, each of these characters believes in the possibility of starting anew, thus escaping the tyrannical enslavement of an economic or social order. At the same time, each possesses a tragic tendency toward evil or madness, by which he prolongs or reproduces this order. He who would play the angel plays the beast. Thus Oberlus seems chiefly a parody of the American Adam, a monstrous version of transcendentalist self-reliance— and so is Bartleby, in his own way. His retreat to an island appears as an attempted self-emancipation from society, and his tending of a garden refers to a major literary commonplace associated with the theme of wisdom,[258] but Oberlus derails these aspirations and mires them in a new order of domination. Eventually Oberlus is defeated because he cannot free himself from his past; his overweening pride imprisons him in solipsism. In spite of this, he seeks to trade with visitors, to conduct a

---

[258] We find it echoed in Melville's contemporary, Thoreau (see esp. "The Bean-Field," *Walden*, ch. 7).

transaction, however perverted, that is economic and thus ultimately expresses acceptance of community. The essence of Melvillean drama, its profoundly grotesque nature, is enacted by these individuals who mime an unattainable self-transcendence, an impossible personal and cultural redemption. In the universe of "The Encantadas," any vague heroic impulse appears doomed to become a grotesque gesticulation.

Melville thus questions whether individuals can ever affirm their autonomy without throwing it off track at the same time, can ever progress by their own effort in spite of a contingence which is imposed on them. Only that saving and regenerating violence which is fundamentally inscribed in the language of the biblical prophets can open the path to a renewed consciousness of their being. The only possibility of regeneration in *The Piazza Tales* is not in the contemplation of nature—especially a *framed* nature, pacified by esthetic conventions—but in unleashing a violence which tears man away from nature's grip.

In this drama which mocks the pretensions of identity, only those survive who abdicate their personality. This is the case with Hunilla (Sketch VIII), who alone accomplishes her own liberation, and perhaps her transcendence, in the death of her personal identity. Similar to all the other characters at the beginning of her adventure, that is to say defined by her material ambitions, she surpasses her own limits only in the death of her ego. The trials that destiny inflicts upon her (betrayal, widowhood, solitude—and rape is hinted) effect the destruction of her ambitions (her economic goals) and of her idols (the tortoises she hunted for their oil). Amid these sketches depicting man's pretensions to sovereignty over the world or over his fellows, Hunilla is the only one who is motivated by her power over her own passions and not over others. She is also the only one to have recognized the illusory character of power and of liberty. Her story thus emphasizes that one of the narrator's essential identities is the painter of *Vanitas* still lifes. A major seventeenth-century genre, the "Vanity" invited the viewer to ponder the relativity of material things by depicting emblems of the brevity of earthly life, such as an hourglass and bones. These appear in "The Encantadas," as does the statement, "nought else abides on fickle earth but unkept promises of joy" (153).

Only through this annihilation of the individual and his pretensions can a renewal become possible. And although the characters of "The Encantadas," lacking interiority, are impossible to identify with, Hunilla may be the only exception, however tenuous. "Humanity, thou strong thing, I worship thee, not in the laureled victor, but in this vanquished one" (157). The pronoun "one" is somewhat ambiguous. It refers to Hunilla ("this vanquished individual") but, grammatically, could also refer to "victor" ("this vanquished victor"). The *type* of a vanquished person who triumphs in defeat is Christ, who must abdicate his mortal identity to redeem humanity. So Hunilla may be seen as a Christ figure, a phantom of God, the only one in this God-forsaken world. In a world consigned to the grotesque by its lack of transcendence,[259] she reveals the necessity of a form of grace. However, the most explicit Christ-symbol is the cross she sees depicted on the back of her donkey en route to her native Payta (162)—a grotesque figure of the Passion. And, since any account of her future is left in the shadows at the story's end, Hunilla offers only a scant image of redemption, and we may wonder whether, in this uncertain world, this is not just another mirage.

V. The Graveyard of Utopias: America and its Myths

Until the Romantic period, the grotesque was concerned with an anti-realist esthetic, concerned with expressing the fantasies of the imagination—*i sogni dei pittori*. The Romantics saw the genre both as an expression of the supreme truth of dreams and the irrational, and at the same time as the tormented consciousness of reality and history. Thus, Friedrich Schlegel

---

[259] The drowning scene specifically indicates the submersion of the picturesque ("bower," "frame") beneath the grotesque.

considerably extended the accepted meaning of the term, opening it to "the contradictions and searing conflicts of the modern grotesque" when he saw in the French Revolution "the most frightful grotesque creation of the century," uniting, "in a terrible chaos, the deepest prejudices, the most powerful intuitions, to create a monstrous tragi-comedy of humanity."[260] Thus understood, the term applies to these sketches in their clearly political aspect.

1. The Myth of the American Nation

> "...let the inhabitants of the rock sing, let them
> shout from the top of the mountains. Let them
> give glory unto the Lord, and declare his praise
> in the islands."
> —Isaiah 42:11-12

Beginning with Sketch III, in fact, we sense that although "The Encantadas" takes us to faraway islands, the story is also a way of Rock Rodondo appears, rather like the *Pequod* in *Moby-Dick*, as the symbolic home of all the nations of the earth, and therefore also as a metaphor for America. On Rodondo, however, these nations just screech their "demoniac din," quite unlike those who sing the glory of the Lord from their rock in Isaiah. Thus the tumult of Rock Rodondo represents the discordant voices of the unlocatable, unattainable American nation, which, like an encyclopedia, can only amount to the sum of its parts, nothing greater, and not that new and transcendent unity of America's national motto (*e pluribus unum*). In an America divided as never before, Melville rejected any comfortable and reassuring framework, and used the image of the archipelago itself as a powerful metaphor for these Disunited States of America in the 1850s.

---

[260] Iehl 54.

2. The Myth of the Promised Land

The Piazza Tales offers an incisive commentary on America and its myths, notably that of the Promised Land. Not only is the narrator of "The Piazza" a disenchanted Moses for whom all divine manifestation slips away, but this ironic "view from Pisgah" offers only a world of desolation to our gaze, not a promised land.[261] As the paragon of a new beginning, of the re-beginning of History, the episode of crossing the Red Sea and the discovery of the Promised Land served as the *type* of the history of America. The typological interpretation of this capital episode could be used to evoke the manifest destiny of that new promised land, America, "discovered" by a people who thought of themselves as a new Israel. In "The Encantadas," however, Melville turns this imagery against America itself, as a pitiless mirror in which to satirize his target. Amid Melville's comico-heroics, the mention of Daniel Boone deepens the irony and underlines the straw-man buffoonery of national myths by upgrading America's iconic pioneer into an incarnation of Moses himself–in typological language, an *anti-type*.[262] It could not have escaped Melville, moreover, that the biblical story of Moses on Mount Pisgah was not without an irony of its own, since Moses was fated by God to die before reaching the Promised Land he had seen from on high, in a subtle mixture of gratification and pain, of greatness and failure.

Melville reprises this initial mockery of the idea of the Promised Land in a more somber form in the episode of the Dog-King (Sketch VII). The grotesque universe is always a world in chiaroscuro, not in the picturesque sense of carefully controlled, expressive gradations of shadow and of light, but in the sense of an ambiguous and deeply mixed tonality: "Often ill comes from

---

[261] Cf. Landow 1980, 205-31.

[262] Certain artists depicted Daniel Boone discovering Kentucky from the heights, for example William Ranney, *Daniel Boone's First View of Kentucky* (1849). (Cf. Sweeny.)

the good, as good from the ill" (156). Such a philosophy, of course, suits our rebel narrator quite well; at the same time, it does seem to express Melville's deep conviction. In this endless interchange between good and evil, the Dog-King, the hero of a war of liberation, soon subjugates the people whom he had enticed to his utopian vision, his promised land (147). Incarnating the ambiguity of prophet and swindler in a particularly sinister version of the confidence man, this child of the Devil appears as a monstrous figure of the Savior, the prophet who guides humanity toward a better world. He becomes a dictator in his turn, illustrating man's inability to escape from the past (Emersonian self-realization notwithstanding). Melville locates truth in the impossibility of permanent moral progress, in the stammering of history, not in any triumphant march toward the millennium. The half-tone truth is that the march of history is a stumble, that one cannot erase the stigmata of colonialism with impunity, and that there are no real heroes. History for Melville is never the revelation of a luminous and transcendent reality, but a chiaroscuro.[263]

In the episode of the Dog-King, Melville mingles the ridiculous with the terrifying: the pack of dogs is a depiction of the repressive system of autocratic regimes. Staging a battle between men and dogs, this sketch illustrates the confusion of genres characteristic of the grotesque. In "The Encantadas," any new departure, any dream of regenerated society is doomed to fail, perverted into tyranny or anarchy. In a fallen world (127), any renewal turns out to be impossible.[264]

No sooner have they won their battle against the dogs than the rebels fight against each other–like dogs. Many of the

---

[263] This idea finds a particularly vivid expression in Sketch V, in which the frigate Essex crosses a phantom ship that might be either British or American–symbolizing not only the limits of vision, but also the obscure wound left by the separation of the American limb from the British body. Melville here invokes history and its phantoms, just as he does in "Benito Cereno."

[264] Significantly, this world is deprived of seasonal changes (126).

rebels in "The Encantadas" are deserters, avid for liberty and dreaming of improving their lot by occupying the margins of a predatory economy. Melville thus contrives to mitigate our revulsion at these outlaws with a touch of sympathy for a suffering humanity unhappily mired in an existence that borders on the absurd. For the overthrow of the Dog-King brings no change in the course of history; the island passes from an autocracy to a "Riotocracy" (149). Sketch VII expresses Melville's aversion to autocratic excess as well as revolutionary disorder–a reaction to the failed uprisings of 1848 in Europe. This episode also expresses Melville's profound skepticism towards the course of history, which he views as a tragic farce, the burying-ground of multitudes. More than ever, the circus and the vale of tears are one.

Throughout *The Piazza Tales,* Melville disappoints our expectation of togetherness with his ceaseless portrayal of an unthinkable community: Melville's drama is that he could not believe in either the heroic individuality of transcendentalism, nor in any community whatever–one of living humans or that of life itself, as he demonstrates in the discordant population of Rodondo. This community could only be the ironic community of the dead, or that (no less ironic) between the dead and the living, as implied by the frail grave markers and messages throughout the story, more likely to meet with ruin than with their—significantly, anonymous—intended recipients (172).

3. Oberlus: America and the Question of Slavery

The confusion between human and animal that is characteristic of the grotesque symbolizes the ceaselessly renewed combat that leads man to disengage himself from animality and affirm his humanity. One consequence is that the grotesque mode is particularly suited for considering the question of slavery, a practice which poses the question of the definition of humanity.[265]

Half-man, half-beast, Oberlus appears as the grotesque creature *par excellence*, changing all who approach into reptiles. Exhibiting his ugliness as an instrument of negative power, a magical object, he becomes "Lord Anaconda" (166). It is clear that Melville, employing a traditional analogy, uses the deformity of the human body to symbolize that of the political body, and offers a political commentary through the two episodes of Oberlus and the Dog-King. A cruel and buffoonish king, a clownish devil whose attribute is the blunderbuss which he brandishes incessantly, Oberlus provokes not only disgust but also laughter at the chasm between his pretensions and his intellect. Terrible and comical at the same time, Oberlus nicely illustrates Ruskin's definition of the grotesque–"in almost all cases composed of two elements, one ludicrous, the other fearful."[266] Oberlus is the prototype of the confidence man, determined to affirm his sovereignty over his territory and over the rest of humanity in pursuit of his interests. He represents the diabolical intelligence that invented slavery. Resistant to any moral revelation, Oberlus struggles with a black sailor whom he means to enslave, in a scene that combines clowning with devilry, a sinister comedy satirizing slavery in America (165-66).

In the 1850s, the question of slavery had become omnipresent in American life politically and morally. The sketch devoted to Oberlus appears prophetic, because it denounces this abomination, and because it seems to anticipate the unleashing of violence of the Civil War. The skirmishes between Oberlus and the black man dramatize the struggle that was eroding the nation. This little skit, more than any other among "The Encantadas," becomes Melville's indirect means of taking sides and arousing consciences, without preaching or moralizing.

---

[265] So does cannibalism, an important theme in Melville which can appear as the paroxysm of the grotesque.

[266] John Ruskin, *The Stones of Venice* (1851), quoted in Landow 1971, 31.

Far from being the Fortunate Isles to which their name alludes, the Encantadas are anything but a paradise, unless it be the paradise of human illusions. Sterile, deserted, and strewn with ruins and tombs, the islands are the dying place of human ambitions, good or evil. At both a national and an individual level, self-renewal is an impossibility. How could it be otherwise in a nature so manifestly degraded, so cut off from any contact with the origin? These are not Rousseauian islands of happiness, but the graveyard of utopias.

"Keep silence before me, O islands..." –Isaiah 41:1

"The Encantadas" gives us a nightmare world, a world of monsters and slaves, grotesque and violent, over which Mammon reigns supreme. It is a world not only abandoned by God, but deserted by faith. The madness and cruelty expressed in the episodes of "The Encantadas" belong to "some sordid farce," to borrow an expression from Joseph Conrad's *Heart of Darkness*: years before Conrad, Melville plunges us into the shadowy heart of a world in crisis.

Denouncing the illusions of vain and powerless reason no less than man's senseless desires, offering an acerbic commentary on America's founding myths, chastising its abominations and waywardness, Melville in "The Encantadas" is one of the heirs of the prophets of Hebrew scripture: "Old Testament prophecy [is] a scriptural genre that devotes itself as much to diagnosing the spiritual condition of an age as to predicting the future."[267] The discourse of the prophets presents three essential aspects: the denunciation of the abominations of the present, the unleashing of divine punishment, and the visionary evocation of a divine promise. The depth of the crisis evoked by "The Encantadas" can be measured by the absence of any promise of rebirth, any vision of a new covenant. Melville's

---

[267] Landow 1986, 18.

deep skepticism forbade him to elaborate any myth of salvation, which would only be one more ideality.

In a universe of disorientation–historical and metaphysical as well as visual and conceptual–there can be no teleology, and therefore no real prophecy. It is this absence, this truncated prophetic schema, that gives Melville's text its power and differentiates it so clearly from other, more openly prophetic voices. Frederic Edwin Church, for example, saw in the Civil War the playing out of a divine plan which, through the ordeal of a major historical crisis, would restore light to the world. While the Oberlus sketch can be read as a prophetic symbol of the Civil War, Melville views the march of history as chaos, and the rest of his tale does not correspond to such symbolic intention. In "The Encantadas" Melville, unreconciled to the demise of the prophetic promise, can only scrutinize the prophetic promise and expose its emptiness.

With no illusions as to the possibility of human intervention in history's course and the world's fate, Melville is nevertheless not too exhausted or disillusioned to give up speaking the *truth*–an unsettling and exacting truth–and to try, in spite of everything, to save America from itself.

10

Melville's Dream:
An Approach to the
Journal of a Visit to Europe and the Levant

Whatever his particular motivation, Melville in 1856-1857 was clearly following the traditional itinerary of other pilgrims in visiting the high points of ancient (and Renaissance Italian) culture.[268] Properly armed with guidebooks, Melville retraced an oft-told voyage, memorialized by a wide range of travelers; he knew a good deal about it before he ever left the States. Yet Melville was not just one more intellectual seeking confirmation of scriptures ancient or modern, in eternal adoration of the holy sites. On the contrary, his *Journal*[269] evinces such freedom of thought that it is altogether different from the usual hagiography. Quite the contrary, the *Journal* appears overall as Melville's protest against a world whose reality, although it can be viewed esthetically, is to be found elsewhere–in the inhuman, in death. No sooner has Melville, attuned to the picturesque, used a lively touch to convey scenes of everyday life (in Syra, for example) than we are unsettled by the vision of a world deprived of life (67-69). The lands he visits look abandoned, God-forsaken, unhallowed (71-73). Melville remarks their wild and brutal aridity, the scarcity and solitude that seem to comprise their very

---

[268] On Melville's motivation, see Jaworski 1993.

[269] Page references in parentheses are to the edition by H. C. Horsford (Melville 1955). A newer edition by Horsford and Lynn Horth is incorporated into Melville, *Writings*, vol. 15 (Journals), Evanston and Chicago: Northwestern University Press and Newberry Library, 1989.

substance. Even when he specifies colors, the picture will not come alive. In their uniformity and nearly abstract coldness ("bleak yellow," 111), color only confirms the curse that weighs upon the land. With discretion, Melville suggests that the victim of this curse could be the weary traveler: "[The Greek isles] look worn, and are meagre, like life after enthusiasm is gone" (111). Later he is less ambiguous: "Was here again afflicted with the great curse of modern travel–skepticism" (166).

With a few exceptions, this negative tendency gets worse the farther Melville continues his voyage. He revisits Syra on the way from Constantinople to Egypt, and writes:

> Entering Syra harbor, I was again struck by the appearance of the town on the hill. The houses seemed clinging round its top, as if desperate for security, like shipwrecked men about a rock beaten by billows. (109)

> Many of islands composed of pure white marble. Islanders retain expression of ancient statues. (111 note k)

Little by little, men become nothing but castaways,[270] blocks of stone, or else ants crawling upon the earth's surface (or beneath it[271]), in the harsh solitude of an immeasurable universe– as if with the retreat of God (or the gods), all relationships, all proportion are abolished. Entire towns and villages are themselves mere elements of geology: they look like sand banks (121), desert rocks (139), or a quarry (150). Sometimes they are caught up in a geological dynamic, the plaything of geomagnetics (109, 162, 239).

---

[270] Cf. also: "Villages ... midway upon steep slopes as if they had slipped there in a land-slide" (239).

[271] For example, at the cistern of the 1001 Columns at Constantinople (81-82) and at the Holy Sepulcher (148-49).

By the time we reach Palestine, there is no more distinction between the world of the living and that of the dead. Melville's text evokes a race of the living dead, surrounded by its dead and only half-alive itself. On the road to the Saint Saba monastery, Melville comes across a "Bedouin encampment in hollow of high hills–oval–like two rows of hearses" (138). Later during an excursion in the environs of Jerusalem, he describes the village of Siloah: "Village, occupying the successive terraces of tombs excavated in the perpendicular faces of living rock. Living occupants of the tombs–" (143). This, like the Bedouin encampment, is an interpenetration of the living with the dead, more than a vague contiguity. This is a key characteristic for Melville: we need only recall his feeling "the intermingling of life & death" as he travels up the Bosporus (94), or these words written shortly before that:

> In the wide tracks, they cultivate them–garden spots–very rich & loamy–here fell the soldiers of Constantine–sowed in corruption & raised in potatoes. (87)

But he adds thereafter, as if it were still possible to keep death at arm's length:

> –These walls skirted by forrests [sic] of cemetery ... The walls seem the inexorable bar between the mansions of the living & the dungeons of the dead. (87)

From Constantinople to Jerusalem, Melville's vision becomes increasingly dramatic. Indeed, after he has been to the cemeteries surrounding Jerusalem and has described a village built in the midst of cave-tombs, Melville evokes the city erected upon the ruins of earlier eras: "There are *strata* of cities buried under the present surface of Jerusalem" (152).

In all respects, Jerusalem thus appears as a "city besieged by [the] army of the dead" (144). As to the rest of Judea, one might almost add that death itself has not only besieged but attacked and invaded a land henceforth drained of life, petrified:

> Judea is one accumulation of stones–Stony mountains & stony plains; stony torrents & stony roads; stony walls & stony feilds [fields], stony houses & stony tombs; stony eyes & stony hearts. (152)

Reading this beautiful passage, we can see the extent to which Melville composed his journal notes in spite of–and in opposition to–drought, rocks and death. In opposition, Melville liberates words from the prison in which the world confines them; words are the only possible light here, where tombs and homes, both of stone, are indistinguishable, and where eyes and hearts no longer flutter. Indeed, this effort at naming can undercut the basic thesis that everything is uniform ("one accumulation"). These nouns, in close combat with "stony" in each phrase and seemingly losing their dominion even in our imagination, tottering on the brink of nothingness, nevertheless open a space. Here as in Constantinople, a hypothetical process of individuation is in play–that of the traveler, made possible by that of the elements of the "landscape." Yet, unlike the crowd in Constantinople (Melville compares the fezzes to paving-stones), from which the traveler escapes by climbing a tower–and which, as in Cairo, ultimately contained a diversity of figures, the Judean desert is absolutely uniform as to both surface and depth, each rock identical to its neighbor, except perhaps in regard to height. And appallingly, any effort to remove a small stone only uncovers another, more massive one:

> Before you, & behind you, are stones. Stones to right & stones to left. In many places laborious

> attempt has been made to clear the surface of
> these stones. ...But in vain; the removal of one
> stone only serves to reveal there stones still
> larger, below it. (152)

In this utterly two-dimensional, identically and infinitely repetitive world, the traveler is in danger of petrifaction, for he can discern no order or plan, no life. Language alone can introduce distinctions, and therefore also a form of distance, ensuring that the traveler will survive, stammering with rage, hurling each word with hurtful, pummeling violence:

> Barrenness of Judea. Whitish mildew pervading
> whole tracts of landscape–bleached–leprosy–
> encrustation of curses–old cheese–bones of
> rocks,–crunched, knawed, & mumbled–mere
> refuse & rubbish of creation– (137)

Throughout these magnificent pages, the vitality of objects wanes in proportion as the traveler increases in a verbal potency nourished by the menacing silence everywhere. The desert is indeed a vast extent of sterile solitude, metaphorically no less than physically. With his extraordinary accumulation of nouns, Melville insists upon the radical otherness of what he beholds. Words are his effort at individuation, differentiation– and mediation. Confronting the disintegration of the world and the silence of objects that are closed in upon themselves, there remains only the solution of naming, repeatedly naming this absolute scarcity, this absolute deprivation that bears man back to his first moments as if to an anti-paradise comprised solely of the mineral kingdom, where neither moss or vine may flourish: "–No moss as in other ruins–no grace of decay–no ivy–the unleavened nakedness of desolation–" (137, underlined by Melville). The slightest combinations of words become inexorably heavy:

–zig-zag along Kedron, sephucril [sepulchral]
ravine, smoked as by fire, *caves & & cells–
immense depth–all rock–enigma of the depth–*
rain only two or 3 days a year–wall of stone on
ravine edge– (138)

Here we may note the writer's suppression of articles
and verbs (except for the past participle "smoked," significantly
a passive form, like "crunched," etc., in the passage cited
previously); it deprives things of both real individuation and a
situation in time. If a verb were used to express a mode of seeing
something, or an object's mode of being, this would demonstrate
mental activity or will; it would show a successful distantiation
from what is perceived. Inversely, an unmediated consciousness
of something external can use only nominal phrases or even just
nouns, drawn up in their objectivity on the other side of an
insurmountable barrier separating object from subject. As we
know from linguistics, the nominal sentence "asserts a certain
'quality' (in the most general sense) as belonging to the subject
of the utterance, but outside any temporal or other determination
and outside all relation to the speaker."[272] The form of the
"description"–often nominal or adjectival phrases (even though
this is typical enough in a travel journal, often hastily
composed)–is the mark of a separation that is not necessarily loss
or suffering (even though these are not uncommon in Palestine),
but rather is proof, at least, that no particular connection exists
between object and viewer. What is interesting to see, to feel, is
the *passage*, especially in the journal's evocation of the pyramids
(which we will examine shortly)–the fact that the alternating
presence and absence of a verb express changes in the mode of
seeing (from separation to coordination and vice versa), changes
which occur amid the interplay of signs, parentheticals and
recalls–changes that reflect the conflicting relationship between
the objective and the subjective that is overseen by God, who is

---

[272] Benvéniste 137.

the very substance of this experience, this splendid struggle reminiscent of Jacob wrestling with the Angel.

We may also remark that these objects, lacking all individuation and temporal situation, are eternal, changeless. The journal never keeps track of generative time, it shows only time the destroyer, or else (as in Palestine) a fixed, immobile time. The reference to ivy and moss appears again in the passage on the pyramids, which contains a veritable inversion of the Edenic scenario. Here in fact everything takes place as if, in a mirror reversal of Adam's expulsion, God is bringing Melville back to Creation (fully relating to Creation is the only possible paradise). As a result, the desert becomes subtly paradoxical. It is at the same time itself and its opposite, as God may decide.

Melville's telegraphic prose, spontaneously expressive of the shock of perception, rips holes in the verbal fabric. An ellipsis in the text, for example, "materially" introduces absence– the prevailing impression in the Palestine passage. Dashes create a suspension that embodies silence or doubt: questioning.

Nowhere in Palestine do we feel the divine presence, not even at the Holy Sepulcher in Jerusalem, where everything is repugnant to Melville. He finds no sublimity in the desert of Judea, that vast tomb. It is a labyrinthine chaos of ruin and darkness, the haunt of pitiable little men, a place oppressive to the visitor. Black and closed, this place lacks all grandeur, all mystery. Conversely, the interior of the pyramids stimulates an ambiguous shudder, but not this pure and simple revulsion. It is not surprising that Melville concludes his notes on Palestine with extreme irony:

> No country will more quickly dissipate romantic expectations than Palestine – particularly Jerusalem. To some the disappointment is heart-sickening. &c.
>
> Is the desolation of the land the result of the fatal embrace of the Deity? Hapless are the favorites of heaven. (154)

And this is the problem that makes it especially demoralizing to experience Palestine, compared with Constantinople where there was no reason to hope for any divine presence, and with the pyramids where the divine presence was manifest (in its primal aspect–dread and terror, a massive, magical immediacy transcending any question of faith). The land of Palestine is not seen as mediating between man and God, any more than Jerusalem. The desert is not the place where God speaks to man; the presence of many historical and sacred edifices, of scriptural abodes, is not hopeful. How could it be otherwise, we may well ask? How can there· be any correspondence between the physical place and the spiritual freight it carries, even in the mind of one who is saturated in it? In the end, these eternal places are only a cemetery, where the divine presence is manifest only negatively, having withdrawn. This is pure transcendence, so distant, so absent, that the idea of Deity becomes a mockery–its "embrace" rendered with irony, for this promised land is actually promised to desolation–even amid a persistent sense of the absolute, of which Melville seemingly refuses to despair. For the reader who senses, among these jottings, the vertigo of nothingness–challenge, suspension, irony, the temptation of silence or, more rarely, silent rage– Melville's travel notebooks are fascinating. The more so, because their many gaps–even within the discontinuous daily entries–are mysteriously filled as the next entry proceeds to build, stone against stone, its monolith. Melville's relentless utterance, his saying of loss and separation and his striving for contact are deeply moving. A celebration in spite of itself, it is not the expression of a happiness, but the bitter vision of a world which may be either dead or alive–we cannot tell. It is an utterance that is at times rather exhausted, often ironic or disenchanted, more rarely violent, and is expertly capable of repossessing whatever remnants of joy or energy remain beyond the tensions.

* * * * *

Pyramids of a "biblical simplicity."[273] No deciphering. The block.

The cosmos is the only metaphor; to see the pyramid is to be in the world anew. The desert, the sea ("A long billow of desert foreevr [forever] hovers in act of breaking, upon the verdure of Egypt"), the mountains ("Pyramids from distance purple like mountains"). Or if you prefer–since this reality is reversible–the pyramid (with its site) is a metaphor for the world: whale + ocean : pyramid + desert. "Desert more fearful to look at than ocean." The desert is Hokusai's Wave, eternally suspended, menacing–like the pyramid, also suspended–the explosive and geomorphic force of immobility. Desert / verdure = ocean / land. A microcosm–those frontiers which in American literature always have to do with the origin (as in Whitman, Stevens...).

One doesn't *understand* the *Bible*. Hard to interpret. Only general sense may be accessible. Bedazzlement: "As with the ocean, you learn as much of its vastness by the first five minutes' glance..." Pyramid: like the sea *and* like the whale.

Elemental pyramid. Impossible to measure it: rejoins the world, both before ("Might have been created with the creation": extraordinary reduplication!) and beyond ("as long as earth endures some vestige will remain of the pyramids. Nought but earthquake or geological revolution can obliterate them").

Non-Euclidean space. "Looks larger midway than from top or bottom." An infinity of parallels pass through one point. "As many routes as to corss [cross] the Alps." Heading where?

No measure possible–endlessly arising ("Pyramids still loom before me–something vast, undefiled, incomprehensible, and awful": the whale), like the world suddenly present to consciousness in its infinity: the traveler cannot absorb it in its entirety–as opposed to other structures, evoked in gastronomical

---

[273] All phrases quoted in this section: Melville 1955, 117-19 and 123-24.

terms: "After seeing the pyramid, all other architecture seems but pastry."[274]

Hence the indefinite. To say the uncountable, redoubling of words: "Precipice on precipice, cliff on cliff," leaving the articulations invisible, for we cannot see them. No connections, no segments that one can count, but a mysterious and secret linking of planes ("at angles, like broken cliffs") of which the end result exceeds the three dimensions of space: "the massiveness and mystery of the prymds [pyramids]."

Enjoyment which is felt not through a physical representation, but through an interplay of forms and tensions.

On this side of the limit, of the finite, of the continuous, breath keels over–to be one with Breath. "Resting. Pain in the chest. Exhaustion. Must hurry. None but the phlegmatic go deliberately." Summoned. You, Melville. And this fallen one, summoned too?

Only space can account (?) for the pyramid, and not spatial categories ("It is not the sense of heigth [sic] or breadth or length or depth that is stirred, but the sense of immensity that is stirred"). No cardinal points. Space envisaged to the point where it is no longer space, but a feeling of immensity. Physically it is no longer there, no longer locatable, no longer assimilable.

Integral space which is no longer space, but the time of its impression in the body and the mind, denied ("oppressed," "awe," "terror"). The leap. To be or not to be: "Here there is no stay or stage. It is all or nothing."

In the vacancy of time and space lodges the sense of the holy. The situation of the pyramid is transcendence.

The pyramid: as if all weight were integrated–in that respect it is closer to Incarnation. Gives the traveler the feeling of being watched: hyperactive consciousness–feverish or in pain–sees in it the eye of God. The eye was in the tomb and was watching Melville. He is even larger Dead than Alive. The

---

[274] Cf. "castle of confectionary" [sic], 94.

pyramid turns and turns, covering in turn the desert, the cliffs of the mind and the silence of the tomb, like a flash and like a gaze.

Intuition of God, but dissipated in uncertainty and fright, in the twilight of the mind ("awe," "terror" which suspend its power over itself, so that it senses, as when fainting, death's perfume).

A *formidably* lyrical and totally pessimistic passage: sublime.

* * * * *

It is thus impossible to prepare to gaze upon the pyramid: the traveler cannot observe the "monument" from different angles in order to comprehend and appreciate the relations among its different planes, their organic or mathematical unity. The pyramid imposes itself on the traveler because it incorporates its own dimension of time and is not just a configuration in space. With most buildings, in contrast, time intervenes only to allow the gaze to embrace, bit by bit, the whole structure. Time is here the separation which cannot be circumambulated, which gives you or does not give you access to the space of the pyramid: "it is all or nothing" (123), and the pyramid is revealed only to the one who is instantly subjugated by its time, and who, though he may have days to spare, would never see any more of it than this. Decidedly, it is the *monument of the instant* and only those can see it who are able to. But this monument and this instant are themselves dynamic; their pulsation, their rhythm are achieved in our fascinated "contemplation." This instant is outside time; it "lasts" until this world, integral in space, becomes real, so that the traveler lives in a unique space-time–the dazzling space-time of his rejoining the world. Melville, who in his detachment was leaving the world of men[275] and seemed to possess a divine prerogative, is struck down as by a bolt of lightning.

The trip to the Pyramids presents an ontological situation in which being totters on the brink of nothingness. It is significant that Melville becomes dizzy, that another traveler faints, and that an entire procession of spectral beings files past ("Arab guides in flowing white mantles" that Melville compares to angels conducting souls up to heaven[276]). The pyramid is eternally "looming," "dim and indefinite" (123). It is and at the same time it is not, more and not yet, ever here and still to come–interestingly, Melville explicitly refers it to God. The reader, moreover, may see in the misspelling "prymds" an analogy to the vowel-less Hebraic spelling of the divine name. Against this ambiguous background of vacuity and plenitude, a vertigo bears down. This is thus a paradoxical and quasi-mystic encounter with transcendence, an encounter that is undone even as it is achieved, just before the vestige of transcendence will disappear, perhaps for all time–or just before it will persist only in the form of a nostalgia that renders all subsequent experience secondary, that is, *insignificant* (as Melville suggests with his ironic comment that all architecture only looks like pastry after seeing the pyramids, and with his notes on Palestine). As you stand before the pyramids, you are not augmented by beauty, but stripped and negated by the *sublime* at the moment when it seems to admit you.

---

[275] Particularly when he went upstairs, as he often did, in minarets, domes and various other high places: by such flight the confusion of the labyrinth is replaced by an ordered expanse.

[276] 118. There is an echo here of Jacob's vision of a ladder leading from earth to heaven (Gen. 28:10-23).

11

Quest for the Sublime and Rhetoric of Empire in Bradford's *The Arctic Regions*

This collection of essays concludes where it began, in the realm of American landscape art. But now we have entered the twilight of American transcendentalism and the dawn of the era of the mechanical reproduction of images in publishing. In this first decade following the Civil War, as we shall see, the search for the sublime more closely reflects the ideology of manifest destiny, or more accurately the "rhetoric of empire," the discourse of Western colonialism expressed in Victorian-era travel literature.

For much of the nineteenth century public imagination in Britain and the United States was captured by the Polar regions, and especially inflamed by the drama attending the quest for the elusive Northwest Passage and the fate of the Franklin expedition.[277] The pull of the Arctic was fueled by a combination of Romantic expectation and desire for power, and it was both reflected and stimulated by the production of innumerable books and works of art.[278]

The artist William Bradford is one of those who capitalized on the craze for the Arctic. This lineal descendant of Governor William Bradford of Plymouth Colony, who was born in Fairhaven, Massachusetts in 1823, and died in New York in 1892, owed his fame to his numerous paintings of icebergs and

---

[277] See Delgado and Savours.
[278] See the studies by Lopez, Spufford, Harvey, and Pepall.

icy landscapes.[279] My purpose here is not to retrace Bradford's entire career, but to concentrate on the book entitled *The Arctic Regions* that he published in London in 1873, a fascinating product of two realms that fired the public's imagination in the nineteenth century: the polar regions and photography.[280]

In this work Bradford sought to capitalize on the era's fascination with polar exploration and northern landscapes. His desire to depict the limits of the New World invites comparison with that of his colleagues in the American West, both in terms of its esthetics and of its support of imperial ambitions. The most distinctive aspect of this work, however, is its complex articulation of the three media of photography, painting, and text, thus reflecting on the shifting terms of visual representation and professional status brought in by the advent of photography.

The Arctic Regions is an illustrated account of Bradford's 1869 Arctic expedition, his final and most ambitious one. This is a rare book, as fewer than 300 copies were produced.[281] It is also a monumental achievement, forming a magnificent elephant folio volume that includes 141 tipped-in original albumen prints. This landmark in the history of early travel photography and of the photographically illustrated book[282] encapsulates the triumphant mood of the Victorian period. Traveling to the Arctic on a major sketching tour so as to come home charged with new materials and inspiration for future work, the artist arrived fully armed physically with steamer, cameras, pens, and sketchbooks, mentally with colonial assumptions (focusing on visual and ethnographic appropriation and the "progress" arising from colonization), and esthetically

---

[279] For an overview of Bradford's career, see Kugler's biography and Wilmerding (1969 and 1991).

[280] Bradford pursued his interest in Northern landscapes through nearly annual expeditions in the 1860s (1861, 1863-65, 1866-67, 1869).

[281] It is not known if the intended 300 copies were all actually produced (cf. Greenhalgh in Kugler 2003, 84 n 4)

[282] See Gernsheim 1984.

with artistic training and the conventions of the picturesque and the sublime. Beyond that widely shared Victorian framework, however, Bradford's book evinces a complex articulation between the different modes of image making that may testify to a form of anxiety on the painter's part.

A World of Desire

Bradford's Arctic is approached via an exotic gateway: the richly decorated binding of the book. This cover of tooled leather and ornate lettering is an extraordinary work of art in its own right. In spite of its symmetry, the design–whose style brings to mind that of Talbot's *The Pencil of Nature* (1844-46)– is an excellent example of Uvedale Price's conception of the picturesque[283] applied to the art of book binding, because of its intricacy and variety of form and disposition. This frame ensured the ultimate containment of the sublime spectacle of the Arctic by the picturesque. With the scalloped edges of the central medallion, reminiscent of the multifoil arches and bracket-cornices of oriental design, it also reflected the general atmosphere of exoticism surrounding Arctic exploration. The Arctic was paradoxically redolent of Orientalism:

> These wild attendants [Esquimaux in their kayaks], shouting at the top of their voices, and flying wildly about, reminded me of descriptions of the savage Cossacks of the Don, or untamed Arabs of the Desert, in their feats of horsemanship, though the scenes were as dissimilar as the elements on which they sported. (22)[284]

Indeed there is a marked similarity between the

---

[283] See Price 1794.
[284] Parenthetical page references, unless otherwise noted, are to Bradford 1873.

atmospheric phenomena of the desert and of the
Polar seas, especially with regard to the mirage
and to apparent distances. (49)

In this context, the ship's very name, "the Panther," resonates
with a strong suggestion of exoticism throughout the book, as
Bradford himself comes to suggest:

...[the bear] stood looking at us just out of rifle-
range. It was evident that he had never seen a
"Panther" of our species before... (66)

Landscape is always as much a mental as a physical
reality, and the book cover wonderfully captures and symbolizes
the Arctic as dreamland. It testifies to the incredible power of the
Northern landscape to excite the imagination. Documents of
Arctic exploration in the nineteenth century form an endless
chain of words and images haunted by their predecessors. It
seems that each new book or work of art increasingly fueled the
reader or viewer's desire to experience the wonder and beauty of
the Arctic. Impelled to make his trips to the Arctic regions by the
influence of such iconic figures as Elisha Kent Kane, Bradford
right away places desire and fascination at the core of his
enterprise:

From my first essays in painting my tastes have
led me specially to the study of marine subjects.
In this connection a perusal of the "History of
the Grinnell Expedition," by Dr. Kane, and Lord
Dufferin's "Letters from High Latitudes," made
so powerful an impression that I was seized with
a desire, which became uncontrollable, to visit
the scenes which they had described, and study
Nature under the terrible aspects of the Frigid
Zone. (vii)

The innumerable narratives and images of Polar exploration produced in the mid-nineteenth century introduced Bradford and large audiences to the Arctic. In particular, two figures brought the Arctic to life for American audiences. Frederic Edwin Church, America's most celebrated landscape painter, in 1861 painted his monumental *The Icebergs*,[285] which was exhibited to wide acclaim both in the United States and in Britain.[286] Church had a studio in the Tenth Street Studio Building in New York, along with Bradford,[287] who likely attempted to situate himself in the wake of the popularity of Church's subject. The second figure, Elisha Kent Kane, was a famous explorer and author of one of the best-sellers of the nineteenth century, *Arctic Explorations* (1856).[288] Although it is the result of the fascination for the Arctic generated by such gripping narratives as Kane's, this leisure trip offered Bradford the possibility to concentrate on the romance of Arctic exploration. The tourist self-consciously mimics the explorer, and, more pointedly, becomes an entrepreneur capitalizing on the explorer's legacy.

---

[285] Church, *The Icebergs*, 1861, Dallas Museum of Art.

[286] Carr.

[287] Blaugrund.

[288] Bradford's title, "History of the Grinnell Expedition," is imprecise. It can refer either to Kane's *The United States Grinnell Expedition in Search of Sir John Franklin; A Personal Narrative* (New York: Harper. 1853), or to his later and more famous *Arctic Explorations, the Second Grinnell Expedition in Search of Sir John Franklin, 1853-1854-1855* (2 vols. Philadelphia: Childs, 1856), which was illustrated with engravings based on watercolors by James Hamilton. Bradford's reference to Lord Dufferin, the author of *Letters from High Latitudes* (1859), who was Governor General of Canada from 1872 to 1878 (and later became Viceroy of India, 1884-1888) may have to do with his desire to seek the favor of the English aristocrats who were subscribers to the book and prospective buyers of his paintings.

"Solely for the purposes of art"

One of those accompanying Bradford on his trip was the explorer Isaac I. Hayes, a former member of Elisha Kane's crew, who in 1860 had launched an expedition to prove the existence of an "open polar sea," which for most of the nineteenth century was widely believed to occupy the North Pole.[289] That some people persisted in imagining the existence of a warm tropical sea at the North Pole shows that the Arctic regions offered a vision that paralleled the myth of the desert American West as the Garden of the World. The North enticed with a power second only to the American West, which it largely mirrored. Like the American West, the Arctic was both chaotic wilderness and morally redeeming sublimity; it was an object or a place of desire, where one could play out the transgression of human limits. Bradford himself–who also had a studio in San Francisco in the 1870s and painted views of the Yosemite Valley[290]–draws a parallel between the Arctic landscape and that of the West:

> Steering straight in shore we appeared at first to be driving directly on a rock-bound coast, without the least possibility of finding a harbour, but there soon opened the entrance of a narrow fiord which wound backwards between lofty hills, presenting a variety of magnificent scenery which I do not think could be surpassed, or scarcely equalled by any landscape in the world, not excepting the far-famed Yo-Semite valley itself. These cliffs were devoid of any vegetation but lack of it gave to this fiord a peculiar majesty and grandeur. (49)

---

[289] See Hayes (1867). Hayes also published his own account of Bradford's 1869 trip, *The Land of Desolation: Being a Personal Narrative of Observation and Adventure in Greenland* (New York: Harper & Brothers, 1872).

[290] Kugler: cat. 62-64.

Bradford's project indeed evokes that of the famous photographers of the American West, who in the same years accompanied scientific expeditions sponsored by the federal government, the surveys by Clarence King, Lieutenant George Wheeler, Ferdinand Hayden, and John Wesley Powell.[291] Some photographs in Bradford's book, such as "Sandstone Rock at the Entrance of Karsut Fiord" (49), particularly bring to mind contemporary works by Carleton Watkins and Timothy O'Sullivan, whose images enshrined the American West as a mythic landscape.

Bradford's venture, however, both echoed and differed from those expeditions. As an attempt at depicting the limits of the New World it may equally be seen as a frontier story, but it was a privately funded artist's expedition, and as a comparatively short trip it has more to do with the rise of tourism in the latter part of the nineteenth century than with those more scientific ventures.[292] As opposed to the scientific expeditions to the Arctic,[293] it was self-consciously undertaken as an artistic project: "This volume is the result of an expedition to the Arctic Regions, made solely for the purposes of art, in the summer of 1869" (vii).

In the context of nineteenth-century culture, however, artist and scientist were often perceived to harmonize. Thus, a note published in *The Art Journal* of 1872 considers *The Arctic Regions'* "admirable photographs [to be] wonderful as

---

[291] Naef and Wood; Brunet.

[292] This is made clear by the fact that Bradford was accompanied by some paying guests on his 1869 trip, as on several earlier ones. The costs of Bradford's voyage were underwritten by the New York financier and patron of the arts, Le Grand Lockwood (to whom the book is dedicated). Lockwood unfortunately was ruined a few days before Bradford's return, as a result of the financial panic known as "Black Friday" (September 24, 1869).

[293] Discussed in Levere.

geological studies."[294] This reminds us that in the minds of nineteenth century readers and viewers, a book such as *The Arctic Regions* combined geographical record and Romantic imagination, and that Bradford could appear as a Humboldtian figure integrating a search for aesthetic achievement with scientific aspirations. His own statement of his purely artistic aspirations, however, is an indication of a process that gradually led the Humboldtian ethos of the explorer-scientist-artist to be swept away by the increasing specialization of human pursuits: the clearly esthetic focus of the book no doubt indicates a transition to this more specialized form of travel.

Bradford's Technological Sublime

This new form of exploration and travel literature was bolstered by technological advances. Even as it offered views of the sublime Arctic nature, Bradford's book was emphatically the product of the "technological sublime"[295] of a leisure trip aboard a steamer in the high latitudes. The bear hunt narrated by Bradford (62-66), for instance, appears as a technological chase fully using the capacities of a modern steamer to satisfy the hunters' desire for trophies. At this point, the trip entirely parallels modern-day safaris in Africa, as is appropriate aboard a ship called "the Panther." It shows to what extent tourism both symbolized and anticipated other forms of appropriation and exploitation.

Even more central to the book, however, is the technology of vision. At the same time that it offers the grandiose spectacle of the Arctic, photography also celebrates itself. As we leaf through this book and appreciate the artistic qualities of its rendition of the Arctic regions, we cannot help thinking about photographic practice and the technological achievement of photographing the Arctic in 1869–although these

---

[294] Wilmerding 1991, 114.
[295] Discussed by Nye.

were not the earliest photographs of the Arctic.[296] The success of this photographic trip appears as a consequence of the invention of the wet-collodion process in the 1850s, which made taking landscape views a much more practical activity than with the daguerreotype.[297] It was nevertheless a challenging accomplishment, and Bradford does not hesitate to praise the photographers' work and to mention the hazards of Arctic photography:

> This feat was more remarkable than the photographing of Jansen's house at midnight, as in this case the bears and the "Panther" were in motion. The promptitude and knowledge of their profession exhibited by Dunmore and Critcherson were worthy of the highest praise, and may certainly be considered as a most unique exposition of photographic skill. (65)

> "Fortunately no lives were lost. but the boxes containing plates for negatives and the jars of chemicals were utterly destroyed." (31)

Each time they wanted to take pictures, the photographers had to set up a darkroom tent on the ice or on the ship's deck and to carry fragile glass plates and bottles of chemicals in order to process the views promptly. Because of its reliance on technological and chemical processes, photography was often seen as a hybrid of art and science.[298]

---

[296] See Wamsley and Barr.

[297] See Gernsheim. The most dramatic evidence of the practicality of the process was that it allowed its practitioners to document war–the Crimean War by Roger Fenton in 1855, the American Civil War by photographers such as Mathew Brady and Timothy H. O'Sullivan between 1861 and 1865, although these war photographs almost exclusively focused on portraiture.

[298] Green-Lewis 37-64.

While it celebrates the achievement of the new technology of photography, however, Bradford's *The Arctic Regions* paradoxically harks back to a conception of the book as a unique piece of craftsmanship. To some extent this mammoth volume, lushly adorned with tipped-in plates (each an albumen print individually processed), reminds one of Audubon's *Birds of America,* in spite of their different manufacturing processes. It marks the end of an era, before the market was inexorably transformed by the development of photoengraving techniques in the 1880s, which "enabled inexpensive halftone screen reproductions from photographs to appear on the same page as letterpress copy."[299] If Bradford was one of the first to have used photography to illustrate a book on such a scale–following the pioneering publication of fellow Quaker Francis Frith's *Egypt, Sinai, and Jerusalem* (1860)–his achievement still belonged to an era when book illustration was a craft[300] rather than to the new market of inexpensive illustrated books and periodicals that exploded in the late nineteenth century. *The Arctic Regions* thus necessarily addressed an elite audience.

The Arctic as Spectacle

The combined use of the technologies of travel and of vision ensured the possibility of creating the Arctic as spectacle. Quite literally so, for Bradford as early as 1870 used the glass plates from his 1869 voyage for more democratic presentations employing the technology of the magic lantern.[301] This apparatus utilized to project images on a screen allowed the organization of large public events, which could better satisfy the demand of the English and American audiences for "true" representations of the Arctic.

The possibilities offered by photography were used to indulge the public's fascination for the sublime spectacle of the

---

[299] Johnson 213.
[300] Gernsheim 7-10.
[301] Kilkenny discusses a slide-lecture by Bradford.

Arctic landscape. The book's extraordinary set of photographs dramatizes the gaze upon a world observed with intensity and devotion, and the very size of the book aptly echoes the majestic grandeur of Arctic scenes. It offers startling revelations of Arctic nature, its unfolding drama and continuing lyric. An eerie stillness reigns in these scenes: human figures, if they appear at all, are minuscule, suspended in the sweep of raw nature. Bradford voices a blend of ecstasy and dread before what he calls "the terrible aspects of the frigid zone" (vii). He expresses wonder at visions in which the inert material transcends itself, bringing a sense of awe which relates them to the esthetics of the sublime, the primary idiom of Arctic representations[302]:

> Gazing upon such a scene, although illuminated by the midnight sun, the sense of solitude and desolation made a tremendous impression on me. No living thing was visible: neither bird, nor beast, nor insect. The unbroken silence was stifling, for none of us were inclined to talk; I could hear the pulsations of my heart; a species of terror took hold of me... (70)

Hayes's *Open Polar Sea* offered a passage which similarly resorted to the conventional language of the sublime:

> There is no cry of bird to enliven the scene; no tree, among whose branches the winds can sigh and moan. The pulsations of my own heart are alone heard in the great void; and as the blood courses through the sensitive organization of the ear, I am oppressed as with discordant sounds. Silence has ceased to be negative. It has become endowed with positive attributes. I seem to hear and see and feel it.[303]

---

[302] See Loomis.
[303] Hayes.

Bradford also celebrates the sublime display of the aurora borealis, and of icebergs, which have a virtual dimension to them which makes them tower between the real and the imaginary:

> From the water's edge, it presents a nearly perpendicular wall..., with countless irregularities, forming weird and fantastic shapes, which appear like the work of some Titanic sculptor, and affording fancy a full scope. Forms resembling those of animals, birds, and fish, with strange contortions of "the human face divine," could be readily traced, and the artist might there find subjects of study for a lifetime. (28)

As this description of an iceberg indicates, the book's literary and artistic renditions of the Arctic regions also appear as dependent on the esthetics of the picturesque and its creation of "views" of ruined buildings or of expressive natural features. When Bradford went to photograph and sketch the remains of ancient buildings of Greenland (23), he self-consciously worked in the tradition of the painter of views. This tradition especially flourished in eighteenth-century Italy, where *vedute* (views) of Roman antiquities in the manner of Piranesi, for instance, with their descriptive precision and secure framing, were meant to satisfy tourist demand. Picturesque views of ruined buildings–or of icebergs, which for this purpose are simply a flickering architecture of ice seemingly adorned with *grotesques*–offered a reminder of human transience, thus sharing the same moral intent as more sublime views, which emphasized human smallness.

Resorting to traditional esthetic models permits one to make sense of things seen and thus to "civilize" nature. However, Bradford repeatedly emphasizes how Arctic nature defies verbal description and artistic rendition, and even eludes definition:

> ...words cannot describe it, neither can the pencil reproduce the grandeur and immensity of the scene, while the camera, with all its truthfulness to nature, falls far short. (70)

Although emphasis on the inadequacies of all literary and artistic media to fully express perception and consciousness were a traditional test and expression of sublimity, Bradford consistently articulates or mediates a sense of distance from the inaccessible landscape, which culminates in his frantic embrace of the ice, voicing his anguish and delight at being confronted with a blank surface that challenges him and magnifies his solitude, his nothingness:

> "Leaving the others to their various pursuits, I wandered, sketch-book in hand, on my particular mission. But there were so many elements of novelty around me to attract or distract the attention, it was difficult to do more than sketch some outlines, which possibly may be reproduced at some future day. At length, I became so fascinated by the scene that I actually threw myself upon the ice, the more absolutely to enjoy it. [...] I was far away from my companions, with nothing to connect me with any living thing. Never before could I imagine or be impressed with such a perfect feeling of solitude." (36-37)

In these lines that parallel Henry David Thoreau's famous "Contact! Contact!" passage in "Ktaadn,"[304] Bradford appears to

---

[304] Thoreau 1972, 71.

be confronted with the invisible wall of things. Craving for oneness with nature, he physically tries to capture what eludes him in an apocalyptic contact with ice, drawn to a void where unprocessed sensation offers a substitute for mystical oneness with nature. Through this action that literalizes Thoreau's desire for contact and somewhat parallels the equally famous "strange thrill of savage delight" when he was "tempted to seize and devour" a woodchuck by Walden Pond,[305] Bradford, forsaking a typically Victorian sense of specter, filling the mind with the overpowering consciousness of universal death, "proclaiming the end of all things, and heralding the everlasting future. Its presence is unendurable." (226).

Visions of Empire

In spite of such a wildly unsettling encounter with a world that offers both threat and erotic allure, being esthetically and psychologically equipped with the notions of the sublime and the picturesque generally enabled nineteenth-century travelers to contain what they saw, and often ultimately fostered their imperial vision. The artistic achievement of Bradford's book should not make us overlook its participation in the discourse of Western colonialism.[306] Bradford responded to the demands of a Victorian audience, offering them both the images they were eager to see and the messages they wanted to receive. Travel was meant to confirm and validate one's world view, and visual conquest symbolized and prepared other forms of domination.

The discourse of domination actually begins with the traveler's conformity to colonial respectability: Bradford visits holders of official prerogatives and cultivates social connections. The semi-official character of his trip is typical of colonial travel: Bradford was less involved with the life of the

---

[305] Thoreau 1971, 210.
[306] As discussed notably by Said and Spurr.

country than with the life of those who ruled it, however
comparatively close to the rest of the population. For Bradford
and his companions the settled part of Greenland was first and
foremost a world of governors' houses and ruins of ancient
times, not a living community, exemplifying Barthes's
contention that in picturesque travel "the human life of a
country disappears to the exclusive benefit of its
monuments."[307] The first chapter is entirely devoted to the
antiquities of Greenland, thus bowing to the long-established
tradition of travel and travel writing as a means to acquire
"culture":

> [The Danish Governor and I passed] "a couple
> of hours ... very pleasantly in conversation
> regarding Greenland traditions and antiquities."
> (17)

The country's past history, as evidenced by these remains,
legitimized present appropriation. In Greenland as elsewhere,
antiquarian study is linked to a wider form of colonial
appropriation:

> What we saw, however, was the work of human
> hands, relics of the old Northmen; the ruins of
> buildings erected by them more than nine
> hundred years ago. And this was "Krakortok,"
> the seat of the once thriving and quite numerous
> colony. When our boats were hauled up, and I
> stepped within the ruins of the ancient church
> whose history was for centuries buried in the
> darkness of the past, it seemed as if I trod on
> hallowed ground. (23)

Bradford's book throughout confirms the validity of the

---

[307] Barthes 1957, 137.

West's imperial vision and contributes to supporting national claims to foreign lands. Bradford voices widely shared colonial assumptions: his insistence on the dirt and smells of the Inuit echoes the traditional theme of native squalor in travel writing; he celebrates the work of the missionaries and the inevitable "progress of civilization" into out-of-the-way areas. He defines a clear cultural hierarchy and systematically characterizes colonialism in terms of cultural gain:

> Here we found a native... Hans proved to be an excellent hunter, but was morose in temper, sulky and ungrateful, exhibiting the worst traits of Esquimaux character, although he had been converted and partially educated by the missionaries. ...Hans must not be considered a fair specimen of the converted Greenlander; he is not put forward as an example of missionary work in this country. From the school at Jacobshavn many excellent teachers have gone to aid in spreading Gospel truths, and it is in a great measure due to their labours that we find these people so free from many vices common not only in semi-barbarous, but also in civilised communities. (80-81)

Bradford expresses a feeling of moral superiority toward the local population and emphasizes the benefits of colonial occupation. He consistently distances himself and the reader from the natives, and intimates that their world should be viewed from the vantage point of Euro-American social and religious assumptions. In this sense *The Arctic Regions* is characteristic of the Victorian sensibility and its consideration of the exotic Other, one variety of whom was the savage. Both esthetically and anthropologically the North was but a more radical version of the West. The stereotypical Euro-American views of Eskimos or Inuits paralleled those of Indians in the

American West at the same time.[308] *The Arctic Regions* offers little or no understanding of the real nature of native culture, whose depiction is divided between a search for the picturesque–like Bradford's description of the way kayaks are made or birds hunted–and a curt dismissal.

Throughout the book, emphasis is unashamedly on scenery, with local people absent except when they provide picturesqueness in a composed scene. So the tourist, as Buzard writes, turns "a real continent into mere pictures." Bradford's writing and camera work are limited to recording the outward evidence of exotic people for Euro-American audiences. Although the photographs go beyond the mere creation of racial stereotypes, they tend to reduce the complexity of Inuit culture to a few readily identifiable and consumable symbols.

Photography, as it captures only an image of persons and objects, may appear as comparatively harmless, but *taking* pictures appears as a symbol of or a precedent for other forms of acquisition, and we know that some peoples thought that it also took away the soul, as Bradford himself was aware. *The Arctic Regions* includes an extraordinary photograph of an Inuit staring at the camera, with the caption: "Esquimaux wide awake. He kept his eye on the camera while being photographed, expecting it would go off or hurt him in some way." (85) The dramatic expression of his gaze perfectly conveys the unease or even terror generated by the aggressive contact between photographer and native; in other photographs Esquimaux avert their eyes from the lens. Significantly, you not only *take* pictures but you *shoot* them. Photography has a predatory nature that parallels hunting–"image-hunter" is a popular way of referring to a photographer–and photographs are not necessarily what Bradford calls "harmless shot[s]" (65) but a powerful tool for creating objects.

The subject / object duality and the process of objectification are essential tools for subjugating foreign lands.

---

[308] Cf. Schimmel.

Objectification backs up appropriation. Bradford's trip was a collecting tour: the aim was to collect both views and objects, which became decontextualized as museum pieces. Bradford describes how some of the crew members' search for skulls of Inuits was checked by the local population (37). This particularly cruel bone-hunting is the most extreme expression of how travelers are often tempted to regard exotic cultures as curiosities. The exotic gaze is more interested in objects, which it terms primitive, than in the men and women who made them, who in their turn appear to be objects–all the more so when they did not make these objects, but actually *were* the *persons* whose bodies have become objects for the colonial collector.

Estheticization also contributes to the "rhetoric of empire."[309] One essential aspect of Bradford's trip is that it was both motivated and framed by earlier descriptions of the Arctic. Time was thus to be employed not to get a better understanding of the region, but to get the best views of it–i. e., the most marketable. One of the forms taken by estheticization is the fact of seeing one place in terms of another:

> It was a winter scene, white, stern, and cold. To the right of this towered a higher and more precipitous mound, surmounted by a wall with watch-towers at short intervals, which would pass for a representation of some old feudal keep, or a castle on the Rhine. Another, standing alone, rose above all the rest, forming nearly a perfect model of the Coliseum at Rome. Others appeared like ruined castles, one in particular having a low wall in front which might have enclosed a court-yard. On this wall were four pagoda-shaped towers, between two of which a breach had been made by the waters, and through it the waves were dashing into a circular

---

[309] For a study of this concept, see Spurr.

basin resembling the crater of a volcano, sufficiently large to contain three or four. (45)

Slowly [dark fog-banks] rolled around the iceberg's base, then gradually rising they enveloped the crest, reminding me of the Laocoon in the serpent's coil. (43)

Drawing comparisons between the Arctic scenery and such familiar wonders of the world and cultural masterpieces as the ancient Greek sculpture of Laocoon, the Coliseum, or the Egyptian pyramids (45, 49) both estheticizes what is seen and imposes external meaning on it, thus amounting to a form of cultural appropriation.

Finally, eroticization is an important aspect of much travel writing of the colonial era and beyond: a covert eroticism has often been one of the pleasures of the exotic. Bradford repeatedly alludes to the attractiveness of some of the native girls, and the balls organized at several ports during Bradford's voyage were occasions for ambiguous mixup–which is a long way from mutual understanding. The voyage of the "Panther" to the Arctic Regions was an all-male pleasure trip, and travel appears as an opportunity for the pursuit of pleasure or as an outlet for repressed sensuality. Bradford's trip, however, is typically Victorian in the sense that it has less to do with transgressing the limits than with testing the limits of transgression.

Negotiating an Artistic Persona: Bradford and Photography

Until this point, *The Arctic Regions* has straightforwardly been referred to as "Bradford's book." But who actually authored Bradford's book? I would now like to consider how different and competing modes of representation are constructed within *The Arctic Regions*. In this respect I will examine the ways in which this work establishes an implicit dialogue between various media–writing, photography, and (unrepresented but omnipresent) sketches and paintings[310]– which run parallel or counter to one another, thus creating a complex literary and visual scene, and reflecting on the change in visual language and artistic status brought in by the use of photography.

My contention is that Bradford's book should be analyzed in terms significantly different from those defined by Carol Armstrong in her thoughtful study of Francis Frith's illustrated travelogue of 1858-59, *Egypt and Palestine Photographed and Described.*[311] Armstrong reads Frith's work through the epistemological framework of photography's participation in the representational system supported by scientific positivism. In that perspective, photography is the primary evidence–providing both demonstration and authentication–which the accompanying text is made to mirror, thus producing the overall coherence of text and image in the book. I believe that the image-text relationship is largely different in *The Arctic Regions,* insofar as Bradford instead uses writing to define his status as an artist negotiating between competing modes of image making.

The Arctic Regions unites, but does not synthesize, the different textual and visual media. The complexity of the full title is itself an indication of the currents of tension within the book: *The Arctic Regions, Illustrated with Photographs Taken on an Art Expedition to Greenland, with Descriptive Narrative by the Artist.* The convoluted title clearly defines this work as an illustrated book, as opposed to a portfolio of individual prints, but the reader is left to wonder about the real articulation of the different realms so awkwardly juxtaposed: narration, description, illustration, art, photography. On the threshold of a

---

[310] Bradford returned from his three-month voyage with between three and four hundred photographs, over seventy oil sketches, and two hundred pencil drawings (Kugler 27).

[311] Armstrong 284-332.

vicarious foray into the Arctic regions, one is faced with the ambiguous identity of an artist turned writer and possibly photographer.

Modern-day readers are likely to infer from such a title that the artist is the one who took the photographs, and that the "art expedition" indeed consisted in taking photographs, since we are now accustomed to considering photography as an art form in its own right. But thirty years after its invention, the status of photography was still controversial, as practitioners of more traditional art forms tended to adhere to academic distinctions that confined them to separate hierarchical orders. However, if the title page is somewhat ambiguous, the narrative leaves no doubt as to the fact that "the artist" was actually the one who conducted an "art expedition" that included, but was distinct from, photographic practice: the book is throughout haunted by the ghost of painting even as it displays and celebrates the achievement of photography.

In Bradford's time photographic images were not the property of those who produced them, but of the photographers' employers, who retained permanent rights to the product of their labor. This created a confusion of authorship characteristic of nineteenth-century photography and typically exemplified by *The Arctic Regions*: although photographs are the predominant feature of the book, the identity of the photographers John L. Dunmore and George Critcherson, professionals from J. W. Black's studio in Boston who came at Bradford's expense, is acknowledged only in the foreword and then late in the text (33, 65), while Bradford assumes sole authorship of the book on the title page and in the dedication to his patron.[312] Furthermore, recent research has shown that thirteen of the photographs in *The Arctic Regions* were actually taken by William H. Pierce,[313] who was Bradford's photographer on the latter's 1864 trip to the

---

[312] "To the memory of / Le Grand Lockwood / widely known for his generous patronage of the arts / and for his acts of unselfish benevolence / this work is dedicated / by / the author."
[313] See A. Greenhalgh in Kugler 84 n 8.

Arctic, and whose contribution has thus literally been written out of the book.[314]

Such forms of erasure are indicative of the subordinate nature of photography in the eyes of many painters, who did not fully recognize it as an art form, but rather as a mechanical process bounded by its documentary value. The photographer was not yet as respected a person as the traditional artist: he was more a technician than a truly creative individual. Indeed, Bradford instructed his photographers which views were to be taken, and his conventional reference to the "sun-given powers of the camera" (11), as it naturalizes the photographic process, tends to obliterate the photographers' agency and thus to deny them any artistic autonomy. The very notion of the camera as "truthful lens," while seemingly praising photography, is actually fraught with a form of debasement, as it precisely deprives the photographer of the human capacity to create: characterizing photography by "its truthfulness to nature" (70) necessarily downplays the role of human creativity, and the photographer is commended only for his technical abilities in recording a preexisting reality. Artistry was the preserve of the painter, whose hand alone could bring representation to fruitful completion:

> ...the scene could be compared to nothing but the quick-changing views of a kaleidoscope. Nor were the colours wanting to carry out this illusion. From dead white to glossy, glistening satin from the deepest green to all the lightest shades; and from faint blue to deepest "lapis lazuli"; and again, as some lofty berg passed between us and the sun. its crest would be bordered with an orange-coloured halo, in which sometimes prismatic shades appeared. The wild, rugged shapes, indescribable and ever-changing,

---

[314] A portfolio of Arctic views by Pierce is part of the Library of Congress collections.

> baffle all description, and nothing can do them
> justice but the sun-given powers of the camera.
> And even that must fail in part, for until re-
> touched by the hand the glorious phases of
> colour remain unexpressed. (11)

Indeed, in spite of his emphasis on the truthfulness of photography, Bradford actually re-touched some of the negatives, in order to add or modify some elements,[315] thus asserting the artist's compositional rights. Color was also brought forward as a decisive element in which photographs were found to be wanting, and this correlatively defined the superior status of oil painting:

> The scene that presented itself was one that none
> except those whose pursuits call them to the
> Arctic Seas have the privilege of witnessing, and
> one that neither pen nor pencil can delineate.
> The play of light and shade was wonderful. I
> was enabled to procure some of the finest
> studies in color I ever saw. (45)

The fact that the photographic achievement was a joint one enabled Bradford to simultaneously appropriate and distance himself from the medium of photography. Throughout the book Bradford subtly enhances his own standing and cultivates his artistic persona through the medium of writing (the "descriptive narrative"), as when he remarks that "long after my companions had retired, I remained on deck alone sketching the midnight sun in its various phases" (63), or that "the scene possessed such rare interest and charm for me that I desired to enjoy it alone" (43). Bradford consistently distances himself from his companions: "I could have remained there wrapped in admiration for an indefinite length of time, but my companions began to give

---

[315] See A. Greenhalgh.

sundry plain hints about dinner, and I yielded." (25) He stands both aside from, and above them, emphasizing fullness of experience and his emotional and creative responsiveness to the pull of the Arctic, as opposed to the more mundane activities of hunting and photography, which can both be referred to as *shooting*:

> As the sportsmen gathered on the forecastle, rifles in hand, the photographers, who had been mysteriously absent below for some minutes, came hurrying on deck with their instruments, and requested the privilege of taking a harmless shot on their own account. The camera was arranged. and in a few seconds the group of bears was indelibly stamped upon the plate (65).

Bradford highlights the spiritual inertia of his companions, who seem to be impervious to the regenerative powers of Arctic nature, and establishes his own artistic persona as seemingly performing nothing but the basic miracle of being and the delicate art of sketching, while the rest of the crew enjoys a predatory relationship with nature–mostly shooting and collecting–or a mechanical contact through an art form–photography–which is celebrated and envied, but ultimately regarded as a subordinate technique, a "skill" and "profession":

> The promptitude and knowledge of their profession exhibited by Dunmore and Critcherson were worthy of the highest praise, and may certainly be considered as a most unique exposition of photographic skill. (65)

The primary purpose of Bradford's use of photography was actually to document the trip for the painter, who would use the photographs to compose his later pictures, following a method of painting that had gained currency in the practice of such painters as Frederic Edwin Church and Albert Bierstadt[316]– with whose work Bradford was familiar[317] – and was also adopted by Thomas Eakins from the 1870s onwards.[318] Publishing a book illustrated with photographs of his Arctic expedition was to a large extent a side aspect for Bradford. The circumstances for the publication of this book[319] suggest that Bradford considered it to be as much an advertisement for his paintings as a celebration of photographic achievement, and the construction of his persona through his narrative testifies to his being concerned with appropriating photography so as to further his own artistic ambitions, but without compromising his status as an artist. The English patrons who were wealthy enough to subscribe to Bradford's book–including Queen Victoria herself among other royalty and aristocracy–were prospective customers for painted views inspired by the photographic prints, which could work as a repository for entire compositions or elements later to be combined in a freely elaborated painting, as indicated by Bradford's practice as a painter and his own statement in an 1884 interview:

> Why, my photographs have saved me eight or ten voyages to the Arctic regions, and now I gather my inspirations from photographic subjects.[320]

Esthetic hierarchies long privileged the easel painting executed in oil over all other media, thus confining sketches to a non-artistic status that only began to be revised during the

---

[316] See Lindquist-Cock.
[317] For several years Bradford had a studio in New York in the Tenth Street Studio Building, along with Church and Bierstadt. (See Blaugrund.) Moreover, the latter also came from New Bedford and went on sketching excursions with Bradford.
[318] See Tucker and Gutman.
[319] Cf. Kugler 30-31.
[320] Bradford 1884, 8, cited in Spassky, 165.

nineteenth century.[321] If sketching appears as the preserve of the artist in *The Arctic Regions,* we should indeed note that sketches and drawings, like photographs in this respect, were traditionally not regarded as autonomous achievements, but as a subordinate technique leading to the more desirable end of an oil on canvas – "I secured some fine studies for future paintings." It is thus the paradoxical nature of this masterpiece of the photographically illustrated book that it adheres to the traditional hierarchical roles and functions of visual media, extending the minor status of sketching to photography. A further paradox is that few of Bradford's paintings managed to emulate the freshness and directness of drawing's "sensation," and that modern viewers tend to be more sensitive to the intimate silence of the photographic images than to the more rhetorically constructed canvases, such as *Sealers Crushed by Icebergs.*[322]

Throughout *The Arctic Regions,* although the power of photography is celebrated, the reader senses that Bradford has contradictory feelings towards photography–mixing fascination with suspicion. Bradford seems to be fascinated by photography because it dramatizes vision and has the capacity to articulate and magnify the alienness of the Arctic landscapes. Photography–in spite of, or because of, its apparent "truth to nature"–appears as an estranging medium: technology both captures physical appearances and estranges man from the natural world. But Bradford is simultaneously impelled by a will to overcome separateness that is achieved through drawing and sketching, and–when these seem to fail him–ultimately symbolized in a radical way by his frantic embrace of the ice. His conventional desire to naturalize photography as "sun-given power" is overturned by his faith in the superior power of human creativity and experience. His embrace of the ice puts forward unmediated experience against the mediate, overly protective use of artistic equipment. Language and sketching, however, although they may prove unequal to the task of articulating the

---

[321] Harvey 1998, 15-22.
[322] 1866, New Bedford (Mass.) Whaling Museum.

sublime experience, somewhat transcend their limitations because they gesture towards the external world, whereas photography encloses it as it fixes movement and essentializes reality. For proponents of academic hierarchies, photography eschews experience, while sketching is on the side of creative experience: whereas you *take* or shoot pictures, you *make* sketches and drawings. Although drawing and sketching do parallel the taking of photographs in the sense that they are subordinate techniques, offering a means of on-the-spot recording that is only preparatory for painting in traditional academic hierarchies, they involve a greater degree of human input. They also provide enjoyment, a term that Bradford never associates with photography. "At length, I became so fascinated by the scene that I actually threw myself upon the ice, the more absolutely to enjoy it" (36): such a statement implies that sketching was a source of enjoyment that ultimately called for "more absolute" experience.

Bradford's embrace of the ice, however, seems to express his dissatisfaction with the inevitable separateness of any artistic approach: it is a radical expression of his desire for a more experiential relationship with nature, as distinct from the instrumental approach of the pen as well as the camera. Although Bradford's experience of the Arctic is by and large organized and regulated by the language of the picturesque and the sublime–which frames the view and teaches us how to see and to feel–the moment when this language breaks down and gives way to his frantic embrace of the ice, though transient, provides a rare and truly fascinating glimpse of a deeper yearning. The disruption of visual norms yields to a primordial relationship to nature, which substitutes a tangible exploration of the world for a mediated artistic experience. The framing power of optics gives way to the erratic power of eroticism:

> ...there was nothing to excite an erratic fantasy
> but while lying thus upon the ice it was
> impossible to divest myself of the idea that I was

gliding along upon the bosom of a placid stream,
which was bearing me imperceptibly onward to
an overwhelming cataract. (36)

Bradford's climactic embrace of the ice is directed as
much against all form of esthetic capture–including his own
artistic practice–as against photography alone. Whereas
Bradford appears to be torn between his pictorial and visionary
imagination, on the one hand, and desire for a faithful
observation of nature, on the other, his apocalyptic embrace of
the ice dismisses both: it runs counter to both epiphanic
sublimation and mechanical absorption. The epiphanic moment,
in its purity, demands self-annihilation, but ultimately confirms
possession. Physical ecstasy, on the contrary, entails true self-
dispossession. It is both quintessentially sublime and signaling
the death of representation, absorbed in physicality.

There is no doubt that William Bradford was a shrewd
entrepreneur self-consciously capitalizing on the nineteenth-
century craze for the Far North, who resorted to traditional
esthetic language to frame and articulate a marketable response
to the pull of the Arctic landscapes. I suggest, however, that
although Bradford never comes close to a profound meditation
on the art and artifice of representation, his narrative stance
brings added complexity to what might appear as a
straightforward celebration of the twin myths of the natural
order and the natural icon. The artist appears to be poised
between the space and substance of the observed world and his
artistic training and aspirations. His laments over the
inadequacies of all media–both artistic and linguistic–to express
the fullness of vision or feeling, although a staple of the sublime
idiom, seem to be tinged with a slight sense of skepticism that
somewhat counterbalances the seemingly absolute self-
confidence of the book. One feels that in *The Arctic Regions*,
however obliquely, almost secretly, Bradford somehow voices
unease or anxiety about the artist's status at a time when
photography had deeply modified the terms and aspirations of

visual expression. His narrative appears to be poised between a dual tendency to consecrate and question the artistic enterprise at the trip's center. Although, on the one hand, he gives Arctic landscapes an iconic value reflected in the magnificence of the book, on the other hand, he seems to deny the possibility for any artistic representation to fully embrace nature, and to suggest that attention to nature is more important than the resulting artistic work–thus partly belying what often appears as the overly triumphant tone of nineteenth-century American landscape art.

215

Bibliography

Adams, Stephen, and Ross, Donald, Jr. 1988. *Revising Mythologies: The Composition of Thoreau's Major Works.* Charlottesville: University Press of Virginia.

Adamson, Jeremy Elwell, ed. 1985. *Niagara: Two Centuries of Changing Attitudes, 1697-1901,* exhib. cat. Washington: Corcoran Gallery of Art.

Armstrong, Carol 1998. *Scenes in a Library: Reading the Photograph in the Book, 1843-1875.* Cambridge: MIT Press.

Avery, Kevin J. 1993. *Church's Great Picture: The Heart of the Andes.* New York: Metropolitan Museum of Art.

Bakhtin, Mikhail 1984. *Rabelais and his World.* (Originally published in Russian, 1965). Trans. Hélène Iswolsky. Bloomington: Indiana University Press.

Barthes, Roland 1957. *Mythologies.* Paris: Seuil.

Beecher, Jonathan 2000. "Variations on a dystopian theme: Melville's 'Encantadas.'" *Utopian Studies,* v. 11 no. 2: 88-95.

Benvéniste, Émile 1971. *Problems in General Linguistics.* Tr. M. Meek. Coral Gables: University of Miami Press.

Bercovich, Sacvan 1978. *The American Jeremiad.* Madison: University of Wisconsin Press.

Bickley, R. Bruce 1975. *The Method of Melville's Short Fiction,* Durham, Duke University Press.

Blaugrund, Annette 1997. *The Tenth Street Studio Building: Artist-Entrepreneurs from the Hudson River School to the American Impressionists.* Seattle: University of Washington Press.

Borst, Raymond 1992. *The Thoreau Log: A Documentary Life of Henry David Thoreau, 1817-1862.* New York: G. K. Hall.

Bradford, William 1873. *The Arctic Regions, Illustrated with Photographs Taken on an Art Expedition to Greenland, with Descriptive Narrative by the Artist.* London: S. Low, Marston, Low, and Searle.

Bradford, William 1884. *Philadelphia Photographer,* Jan. 21, 1884.

Breinig, Helmbrecht 1968. "The Destruction of Faeryland: Melville's 'Piazza' in the Tradition of the American Imagination." *ELH: A Journal of English Literary History,* Vol. 35, no. 2: 254-83.

Brown, Lee Rust 1997. *The Emerson Museum: Practical Romanticism and the Pursuit of the Whole.* Cambridge: Harvard University Press.

Brunet, François 1999. "Geological Views as Social Art: Explorers and Photographers in the American West. 1859-1879," in Jean Clair, ed., *Cosmos: From Romanticism to Avant-garde,* 86-92. Munich, London, and New York: Prestel.

Bryant, John 1991. "Toning Down the Green: Melville's Picturesque." In Christopher Sten, ed., *Savage Eye: Melville and the Visual Arts,* 145-61.

216

Kent, Ohio: Kent State University Press.

Burke, Edmund 1967. A *Philosophical Enquiry into the Origin of our Ideas of the Sublime and the Beautiful* (1757), ed. James T. Boulton. London: Routledge and Kegan Paul.

Buzard, James**Error! Bookmark not defined.** 1993. *The beaten track: European tourism, literature, and the ways to culture, 1800-1918*. Oxford: Clarendon.

Cameron, Sharon 1985. *Writing Nature: Henry Thoreau's Journal*. New York and Oxford: Oxford University Press.

Carr, Gerald L. 1980. *Frederic Edwin Church. The Icebergs*. Dallas: Dallas Museum of Fine Arts.

Chenetier, Marc 1990. "Tinkering, Extravagance: H. D. Thoreau, H. Melville and A. Dillard." in Yves Carlet and Michel Granger, eds., *Confluences américaines: Mélanges en l'honneur de Maurice Gonnaud*, 211-28. Nancy: Presses Universitaires de Nancy.

Cole, Thomas 1965. "Essay on American Scenery" (1836). In John W. McCoubrey, ed., *American Art 1700-1960: Sources and Documents*. Englewood Cliffs: Prentice-Hall.

Collison, Gary 2000. "Emerson and Antislavery," in Joel Myerson, ed., *A Historical Guide to Ralph Waldo Emerson*, 179-209. New York: Oxford University Press.

Cook, Richard M. 1978. "Evolving the Inscrutable: The Grotesque in Melville's Fiction." *American Literature*, vol. 49: 544-59.

Delbanco, Andrew, ed. 2001. *Writing New England: An Anthology from the Puritans to the Present*, Cambridge, Mass.: Belknap Press of Harvard University Press.

Delgado, James P. 1999. *Across the Top of the World: The Quest for the Northwest Passage*. New York: Facts on File.

Derail, Agnès 2000. "Melville, Linné, Darwin: des taxons et des monstres." *Etudes Anglaises*, vol. 53, no. 1, 3-18.

Dillingham, William B. 1977. *Melville's Short Fiction, 1853-1856*. Athens: University of Georgia Press.

Dorman, Robert L. 1998. *A Word for Nature: Four Pioneering Environmental Advocates, 1845-1913*. Chapel Hill: University of North Carolina Press.

Dove, Janine 1992. "Melville's 'Encantadas': Harmony or False Notes," in Viola Sachs, ed., *L 'lmaginaire Melville: A French Point of View*, 65-76. Paris: Presses Universitaires de Vincennes.

Dunmore, J. L. 1869. "The Camera among the Icebergs." *The Philadelphia Photographer* 6:412-14.

Emerson, Ralph Waldo 1978. *Journals and Miscellaneous Notebooks*, vol. XIV, 1856-1861, ed. Susan Sutton Smith and Harrison Hayford, Cambridge: Belknap Press of Harvard University Press.

Emerson, Ralph Waldo 1983. *Essays and Lectures*, ed. Joel Porte, New York: Library of America.

Emerson, Ralph Waldo 1995. *Emerson's Antislavery Writings*, ed. Len

217

Gougeon and Joel Myerson, New Haven: Yale University Press.

Emerson, Ralph Waldo 2001. *Emerson's Prose and Poetry,* ed. Joel Porte and Saundra Morris. New York: Norton.

Fabian, Rainer and Adam, Hans-Christian 1983. "Greenland. A Cheerful Outing Among the Icebergs: Dunmore and Critcherson," in *Masters of Early Travel Photography,* 63-78. London: Thames and Hudson.

Fisher, Marvin 1977. *Going Under: Melville's Short Fiction and the American 1850s,* Baton Rouge: Louisiana State University Press.

Fogle, Richard Harter 1960. *Melville's Shorter Tales.* Norman: University of Oklahoma Press.

Franklin, H. Bruce 1967. "The Island Worlds of Darwin and Melville." *The Centennial Review,* vol. 11, 353-370.

Furrow, Sharon 1973. "The Terrible Made Visible: Melville, Salvator Rosa, and Piranesi." *ESQ,* vol. 19, no. 4, 237-53.

Gernsheim, Helmut 1984. *Incunabula of British Photographic Literature: A Bibliography of British Photographic Literature 1839-75 and British Books Illustrated with Original Photographs.* London and Berkeley: Scolar Press.

Gernsheim, Helmut 1988. *The History of Photography,* vol. 2: *The Rise of Photography, 1850-1880.* 3rd rev. ed. London and New York: Thames and Hudson.

Goetzmann, William H. 1986. *New Lands, New Men: America and the Second Great Age of Discovery.* New York: Viking.

Gonnaud, Maurice 1964. *An Uneasy Solitude: Individual and Society in the Work of Ralph Waldo Emerson,* Princeton, Princeton University Press.

Gougeon, Len 1990. *Virtue's Hero: Emerson, Antislavery, and Reform,* Athens, University of Georgia Press.

Gould, Stephen Jay 1989. "Church, Humboldt and Darwin: The Tension and Harmony of Art and Science." In Franklin Kelly, ed., *Frederic Edwin Church,* 94-107. Washington: National Gallery of Art.

Granger, Michel 1994. "Le detour par le non-humain," in M. Granger, dir., *Henry D. Thoreau,* p. 232-246. Paris: l'Herne.

Green-Lewis, Jennifer 1996. *Framing the Victorians: Photography and the Culture of Realism.* Ithaca: Cornell University Press.

Gysin, Fritz 1975. *The Grotesque in American Negro Fiction: Jean Toomer, Richard Wright, and Ralph Ellison.* Bern: Francke.

Harvey, Eleanor Jones 1998. *The Painted Sketch: American Impressions from Nature, 1830-1880.* Dallas: Dallas Museum of Art; New York: Harry N. Abrams.

Harvey, Eleanor Jones 1999. "The Artistic Conquest of the Far North," in Jean Clair, ed., *Cosmos: From Romanticism to Avant-garde.* Munich, London, and New York: Prestel, 108-13 and 119-41.

Hawthorne, Nathaniel 1982. "My Visit to Niagara" (1835). In *Tales and Sketches,* ed. Roy Harvey Pearce. New York: Library of America.

Hayes, Isaac Israel 1867. *The Open Polar Sea: A Narrative of a Voyage of*

Discovery Towards the North Pole, in the Schooner "United States,"
New York: Hurd and Stoughton.

Horch, Frank 1973. "Photographs and Paintings by William Bradford,"
American Art Journal 5.2: 61-70.

Howarth, William 1982. *The Book of Concord: Thoreau's Life as a Writer.*
New York: Viking Press.

Humboldt, Alexander von, and Bonpland, Aimé de 1852. *Personal Narrative of
Travels to the Equinoctial Regions of America, during the Years 1799-
1804,* trans. Thomasina Ross. London: Henry G. Bohn.

Humboldt, Alexander von 1860. *Cosmos: A Sketch of a Physical Description of
the Universe,* trans. E.C. Otté. New York: Harper & Brothers.

Huntington, David 1980. "Church and Luminism: Light for America's Elect."
In John Wilmerding, ed., *American Light: The Luminist Movement, 1850-
1875,* exhib. cat. Washington: National Gallery of Art.

Iehl, Dominique. 1997 *Le grotesque,* Paris, Presses Universitaires de France.

James, William 1907. *Pragmatism: A new name for some old ways of
thinking.* New York: Longman Green.

Jaworski, Philippe, ed. 1993. Herman Melville, *Carnets de Voyage (1856-
1857).* Paris: Mercure de France.

Jaworski, Philippe 1986. *Melville. Le désert et l'empire.* Paris: Presses de
l'Ecole Normale Supérieure.

Kant, Immanuel 1982. *Critique of Judgment* (1790), French trans. Paris: Vrin.

Kant, Immanuel 1980. *Critique of Pure Reason* (1781), French trans. Paris:
Presses Universitaires de France.

Karcher, Carolyn L. 1980. *Shadow over the Promised Land: Slavery, Race, and
Violence in Melville's America,* Baton Rouge: Louisiana State University
Press.

Kayser, Wolfgang 1981. *The Grotesque in Art and Literature,* trans. Ulrich
Weisstein. New York: Columbia University Press.

Kelly, Franklin, and Carr, Gerald L., 1987. *The Early Landscapes of Frederic
Edwin Church, 1845-1854,* exhib. cat. Fort Worth: Amon Carter
Museum.

Kelly, Franklin 1989. *Frederic Edwin Church.* Washington: National Gallery
of Art, Smithsonian Institution Press.

Kilkenny, Anne-Marie Amy 1994. "Life and scenery in the far north: William
Bradford's 1885 lecture to the American Geographical Society."
American Art Journal vol. 26 no. 1-2: 106-108.

Koster, Donald 1975. *Transcendentalism in America.* Boston: Twayne.

Kugler, Richard C. 2003. *William Bradford: Sailing Ships and Arctic Seas.*
With contributions by Erik A. Ronnberg and Adam Greenhalgh. New
Bedford: New Bedford Whaling Museum.

Landow, George P. 1986. *Elegant Jeremiahs: The Sage from Carlyle to Mailer.*
Ithaca: Cornell University Press.

Landow, George P. 1971. *The Aesthetic and Critical Theories of John Ruskin.*
Princeton: Princeton University Press.

Landow, George P. 1980. *Victorian Types, Victorian Shadows*, Boston: Routledge & Kegan Paul.

Lebeaux, Richard 1984. *Thoreau's Seasons*. Amherst: University of Massachusetts Press.

Leopold, Aldo 1949. *A Sand County Almanac*. London and New York: Oxford University Press.

Levere, Trevor H. 1993. *Science and the Canadian Arctic: A Century of Exploration 1818-1918*. Cambridge and New York: Cambridge University Press.

Leyda, Jay 1969. *The Melville log; a documentary life of Herman Melville, 1819-1891*. New York: Gordian Press.

Lindquist-Cock, Elizabeth 1977. *The Influence of Photography on American Landscape Painting, 1839-1880*. New York: Garland.

Loomis, Chauncey C. 1977. "The Arctic Sublime," in U. C. Knoepflmacher and G. B. Tennyson, eds., *Nature and the Victorian Imagination*, 95-112. Berkeley: University of California Press.

Lopez, Barry 1986. *Arctic Dreams: Imagination and Desire in a Northern Landscape*. New York: Bantam.

MacCannell, Dean 1976. *The Tourist: A New Theory of the Leisure Class*. New York: Schocken.

Malaurie, Jean 2000. *Ultima Thule: de la découverte à l'invasion*. Paris: Editions du Chêne.

Manwaring, Elizabeth W. 1965. *Italian Landscape in Eighteenth-Century England: A Study of the Influence of Claude Lorrain and Salvator Rosa on English Taste, 1700-1800*. London: F. Cass.

Marien, Mary Warner 1999. "First Images of Yosemite, First Icons of the American West," in Jean Clair, ed., *Cosmos: From Romanticism to Avant-garde*. Munich/London/New York: Prestel, 80-84.

Maynard, William Barksdale 1999. "Thoreau's House at Walden," *Art Bulletin*, vol. 81, no. 2, 303-25.

Meindl, Dieter 1996, *American Fiction and the Metaphysics of the Grotesque*. Columbia: University of Missouri Press.

Melville, Herman 1955. *Journal of a Visit to Europe and the Levant, October 11, 1856-May 6, 1857*. Howard C. Horsford, ed. Princeton: Princeton University Press, 1955.

Melville, Herman 1971. *Pierre; or, The Ambiguities* (1852). Harrison Hayford et al., eds., Evanston: Northwestern University Press, 1971.

Melville, Herman 1987. *The Piazza Tales and Other Prose Pieces, 1839-60*. Harrison Hayford et al., eds. Evanston: Northwestern University Press, 1987.

Miller, Angela 1993. *The Empire of the Eye: Landscape Representation and American Cultural Politics, 1825-1875*. Ithaca and London: Cornell University Press.

Monfort, Bruno 2004. "Rhétorique et inscription du sujet dans *The Icebergs* de F. E. Church." *Revue Française d'Etudes Américaines* 99, 21-41.

220

Moorhead, James H. 1978. *American Apocalypse: Yankee Protestants and the Civil War,1860-1869*. New Haven: Yale University Press.

Myerson, Joel, ed. 1995. *The Cambridge Companion to Henry David Thoreau*Error! *Bookmark not defined.*. Cambridge (UK): Cambridge University Press.

Naef, Weston J. and Wood, James N. 1975. *Era of Exploration: The Rise of Landscape Photography in the American West, 1860-1885*. Buffalo: Albright-Knox Gallery.

Nash, Roderick 1982. *Wilderness and the American Mind*. New Haven: Yale University Press.

Neufeldt, Leonard N. 1995. "Thoreau in his Journal," in Joel Myerson, ed., *The Cambridge Companion to Henry David Thoreau*, 107-23, Cambridge (UK): Cambridge University Press.

Newberry, Ilse 1966. "'The Encantadas': Melville's Inferno." *American Literature*, Vol. 38, 49-68.

Norton Anthology of American Literature. Nina Baym et al., eds. New York: Norton, 1994.

Novak, Barbara 1980. *Nature and Culture*. London: Thames and Hudson.

Nye, David E. 1994. *American Technological Sublime*. Cambridge, Mass.: MIT Press.

Pascal, Blaise 1952. *Pensées* and *The Provincial Letters*. New York: Random House.

Peck, H. Daniel, ed. 1993. *A Year in Thoreau's Journal: 1851*. Harmondsworth: Penguin.

Peck, H. Daniel 1990. *Thoreau's Morning Work: Memory and Perception in* A Week on the Concord and Merrimack Rivers, *the Journal, and* Walden. New Haven: Yale University Press.

Pepall, Rosalind 1999. "Icebergs, Polar Bears and the Aurora Borealis," in Jean Clair, ed., *Cosmos: From Romanticism to Avant-garde*, 114-18. Munich, London, and New York: Prestel.

Phillips, Sandra S. 1983. "The Arctic Voyage of William Bradford: Photographs by John Dunmore and George Critcherson under the Direction of William Bradford," *Aperture* 90, 16-27.

Price, Uvedale 1794. *An Essay on the Picturesque as Compared with the Sublime and the Beautiful*. London: J. Robson.

Richardson, Robert D., Jr., 1986. *Henry David Thoreau: A Life of the Mind*. Berkeley: University of California Press.

Robinson, David M. 1989. "The Sermons of Ralph Waldo Emerson: An Introductory Historical Essay." In Albert J. Von Frank, ed., *The Complete Sermons of Ralph Waldo Emerson*, vol. 1. Columbia: University of Missouri Press.

Rosenwald, Lawrence 1988. *Emerson and the Art of the Diary*. New York: Oxford University Press.

Said, Edward S. 1978. *Orientalism*. New York: Pantheon.

Sattelmeyer, Robert 1988. *Thoreau's Reading*. Princeton: Princeton University

Press.

Savours, Ann 1999. *Search for the Northwest Passage*. New York: Saint Martin's Press.

Schimmel, Julie 1991. "Inventing 'the Indian,'" in William H. Truettner, ed., *The West as America: Reinterpreting Images of the Frontier, 1820-1920*, 149-89. Washington: Smithsonian Institution Press.

Scott, Jonathan 1995. *Salvator Rosa: His Life and Times*. New Haven and London: Yale University Press.

Sealts, Merton 1988. *Melville's Reading*. Columbia: University of South Carolina Press.

Spassky, Natalie 1985. *American Paintings in the Metropolitan Museum of Art*, Vol. II. Princeton: Princeton University Press.

Specq, François 1995. *Le savant, le poète et le jardinier: Le Journal de Thoreau et la condition poétique*. Doct. diss. Paris: Université Paris 7.

Specq, François, tr. and ed. 2004. Thoreau, H. D., *Les Forêts du Maine*, Paris: Editions Rue d'Ulm.

Spufford, Francis 1999. *"I May be Some Time": Ice and the English Imagination*. New York: Picador.

Spurr, David 1993. *The Rhetoric of Empire: Colonial Discourse in Journalism, Travel Writing, and Imperial Administration*. Durham: Duke University Press.

St. Armand, Barton Levi 1986. "Melville, Malaise, and Mannerism: The Originality of 'The Piazza.'" In *Perspective: Art, Literature, Participation*, ed. Mark Neuman and Michael Payne, 72-101. Lewisburg: Bucknell University Press.

St. Armand, Barton Levi 1997. "The Book of Nature and American Nature Writing: Codex, Index, Contexts, Prospects." *ISLE (International Studies in Literature and the Environment)* vol. 4, no. 1, 29-42.

Stein, William Bysshe 1960. "Melville's Comedy of Faith." *English Literary History*, vol. 27, no. 4, 315-33.

Stevens, Wallace 1981. *Complete Poems*. New York: Knopf.

Sweeney, J. Gray 1992. *The Columbus of the Woods: Daniel Boone and the Typology of Manifest Destiny*, exhibition catalog. St. Louis: Washington University Gallery of Art.

Thomson, Philip 1972. *The Grotesque*. London, Methuen.

Thoreau, Henry David 1971. *Walden* (1854), ed. J. Lyndon Shanley. Princeton: Princeton University Press.

Thoreau, Henry David 1972. *The Maine Woods* (1864), ed. Joseph J. Moldenhauer. Princeton: Princeton University Press.

Thoreau, Henry David 1980a. "Walking" (1862). In *The Natural History Essays*, ed. Robert Sattelmeyer. Salt Lake City: Peregrine Smith, 1980.

Thoreau, Henry David 1980b. *A Week on the Concord and Merrimack Rivers* (1849), ed. Carl F. Hovde et al. Princeton: Princeton University Press.

Thoreau, Henry David. *Journal*, ed. Bradford Torrey and Francis H. Allen (1906). New York: Dover, 1962.

222

Thoreau, Henry David. *Journal,* various editors. Princeton: Princeton University Press. 7 volumes to date: vol. 1: 1837-1844 (1981); vol. 2: 1842-1848 (1984); vol. 3: 1848-1851 (1990); vol. 4: 1851-1852 (1992); vol. 5: 1852-1853 (1997); vol. 6: 1853 (2000); vol. 8: 1854 (2002).

Thoreau, Henry David 1958. *Correspondence,* ed. Walter Harding and Carl Bode. Westport: Greenwood Press.

Thoreau, Henry David 2002. *Essays,* ed. Lewis Hyde. New York: North Point Press.

Todorov, Tzvetan 1970. *Introduction à la littérature fantastique.* Paris, Seuil.

Tucker, Mark and Gutman, Nica 2001. "Photographs and the Making of Paintings," in Darrel Sewell, *Thomas Eakins*, 225-239. Philadelphia: Philadelphia Museum of Art.

Vaughan, Richard 1994. *The Arctic: A History.* Stroud (Gloucestershire): Sutton.

Von Frank, Albert J. 1998. *The Trials of Anthony Burns: Freedom and Slavery in Emerson's Boston,* Cambridge: Harvard University Press.

Walls, Laura Dassow 1995. *Seeing New Worlds: Henry David Thoreau and Nineteenth-Century Natural Science.* Madison: University of Wisconsin Press.

Wamsley, Douglas and Barr, William 1998. "Early Photographers of the Canadian Arctic and Greenland," in J. C. H. King and Henrietta Lidchi, eds., *Imaging the Arctic*, 36-45. Seattle: University of Washington Press.

Welling, William 1978. *Photography in America: The Formative Years, 1839-1900.* New York: Thomas Y. Crowell.

White, Kenneth. "Henry Thoreau, homme du dehors," introduction to: Henry David Thoreau, *Journal*, 7-26. Paris, Les Presses d'Aujourd'hui.

White, Kenneth. 1981 "Le *Journal* de Thoreau: un chantier de géopoétique," in M. Granger, dir., *Henry D. Thoreau*, p. 274-81. Paris: l'Herne, 1994.

Whitman, Nicholas 1998. "Technology and Vision: Factors Shaping Nineteenth-Century Arctic Photography," in J. C. H. King and Henrietta Lidchi, eds., *Imaging the Arctic,* 29-35. London: British Museum Press; Seattle: University of Washington Press.

Wilmerding, John 1969. *William Bradford, 1823-1892*, exhib. cat. Lincoln, Mass.: DeCordova and Dana Museum.

Wilmerding, John 1991. "William Bradford: Artist of the Arctic," in *American Views: Essays on American Art,* 99-122. Princeton: Princeton University Press.

Index

226

228

About the Author

Francois Specq, a specialist in 19th-century American literature, is Associate Professor at the Université Lumière-Lyon 2, France. A graduate of the Ecole Normale Supérieure, he is the author of a forthcoming translation and critical study of antislavery speeches by Thoreau and Douglass. *Transcendence*, long awaited, is his first book-length publication in English.

The Author's Bibliography includes:

2005 : *"Se perdre de vue dans ce que l'on voit : Le Journal de Thoreau et l'écriture de la nature"*, Revue Française d'Études Américaines *n° 106 (December 2005), pp. 8-18.*

2005 : "L'Amérique selon Frederic Edwin Church", Transatlantica n°4 (May 2005)

2004 : "L'éthique littéraire d'Emerson", Cahiers Charles V (University Paris 7) n° 37 , pp. 45-64.

2004 : "Emerson's Rhetoric of Empowerment in his 'Address on the Fugitive Slave Law' (1851)", Cahiers Charles V (University Paris 7) n° 37, pp. 115-129.

2003 : *"Thoreau's Flowering of Facts and the Truth of Experience", in Beverly Maeder (ed.), Representing Realities: Essays in American Literature, Art and Culture, SPELL (Swiss Papers in English Language and Literature, Tübingen: Gunter Narr) n° 16 (2003): 51-66.*

2003 : *"Thoreau's 'Chesuncook' or Romantic Nature Imperiled: An American Jeremiad", in Hans Bak and Walter W. Hölbling (eds.),* Nature's Nation Reconsidered: American Concepts of Nature from Wonder to Ecological Crisis, *Amsterdam: VU University Press, 2003, pp. 126-134.*

2003 : *"Emerson et le mouvement transcendantaliste", in F. Brunet et A. Wicke (eds.),* L'œuvre en prose de Ralph Waldo Emerson, *Paris, Armand Colin/CNED, 2003, pp. 19-33.*

2002 : "*Du divin au grotesque II : grotesque et prophétie dans « The Encantadas »*", *in Bruno Monfort (ed.),* Herman Melville: The Piazza Tales, *Paris, Armand Colin/CNED, 2002, pp. 144-168.*

2002 : "*Du divin au grotesque I : « Truth comes in with darkness » : transparence et opacité dans «The Piazza »*", *in Bruno Monfort (ed.),* Herman Melville: The Piazza Tales, *Paris, Armand Colin/CNED, 2002, pp. 43-59.*

1999 : "*La demeure et le labyrinthe : Aspects de la présence au monde dans le* Journal *de Thoreau [The Dwelling-Place and the Labyrinth: Some Aspects of Man's Presence to the World in Thoreau's* Journal*]*", *in Yves Carlet (ed.),* Henry David Thoreau, Profils Américains *(Montpellier, France) n°10 (1999): 113-125.*

1993 : "*Le Songe de Melville [Melville's Dream]*", *in Yves Carlet (ed.),* Herman Melville, Profils Américains *(Montpellier, France) n° 5 (1993): 149-159.*